THE ART OF ARCHERY

Other books by the same author

ARCHERY: THE MODERN APPROACH

THE GREY GOOSE WING

A HISTORY OF TARGET ARCHERY

BETTER ARCHERY

BRAZILIAN INDIAN ARCHERY

IN PURSUIT OF ARCHERY
(with C.B. Edwards)

THE ART OF
ARCHERY

E.G. HEATH

KAYE & WARD
LONDON

First published in Great Britain by
Kaye & Ward Ltd
21 New Street, London EC2M 4NT
1978

ISBN 0 7182 1183 9

Set in VIP Palatino by Bishopsgate Press Ltd
Printed in Great Britain by Cox & Wyman Ltd,
London, Fakenham and Reading

CONTENTS

PART FOUR
Variety and Competition

ACKNOWLEDGEMENTS

The majority of illustrations in this book were taken by David Manners, whose patience and understanding of the problems presented by such a work are specially acknowledged. Thanks are also due to Chris Winder, Tom Ransom, Dennis Sayer, Denise Heath, and Trevor and Carol Davis who acted as models, in addition to all those unnamed archers who may find themselves featured in one way or another in these pages in unposed situations. They have helped, albeit unwittingly, to present the true character of archery merely by pursuing their chosen sport.

Grateful thanks are also due to the Right Honourable the Viscount Massereene and Ferrard who generously provided special facilities for photography in the grounds of Chilham Castle and to the Grand National Archery Meeting at Oxford, the Canterbury Archers, the William Somner Tournament at Canterbury, and the Herne Bay Archers, all of whom provided additional facilities. The illustration on page 63 is reproduced by kind permission of Jennings Compound Bow Inc., those on pages 29 and 81 were taken by Michael Wesselink and are reproduced by permission of the Canadian Olympic Games Organizing Committee 1976, that on page 12 is reproduced by permission of *The Times*, and *The Scotsman* has allowed reproduction of those on pages 183 and 191. Other photographs and the cover design are by the author.

Extract from *Rules of Shooting* have been reproduced by kind permission of the Grand National Archery Soci ty. Measurements are sometimes given in imperial and sometimes in metric in accordance with whatever rules are quoted, G.N.A.S. or F.I.T.A.

PREFACE

In the last decade or so archery has enjoyed an international revival undreamed of by earlier devotees of the bow, and this has been encouraged by improvements in shooting techniques and technological changes which have increased scores spectacularly and transformed bows and arrows from traditionally simple weapons into instruments of precision engineering. What has not changed is the archer, who acquires his skills as a result of knowledge and practice in the same way as his forefathers did before him, and who has to overcome the same practical problems as they had.

Four and a half centuries ago, when the bow began to be regarded as a means for enjoyment, distinct from its more grim warlike role, enthusiasts began to set down in print all those things that are necessary to become an archer. Two earlier books bear the title *The Art of Archery*; one, published in Paris about 1515, and the other, dedicated to Charles I, bearing the date 1634. The changes in social attitudes and in the awareness for the need of martial preparedness in the years between those two volumes called for different approaches to the subject. Since then society has undergone radical changes and the contemporary archery scene has altered with it, and so it has been necessary to up-date, modify and improve manuals on shooting with the bow and arrow over the years.

However, some of the principles of archery theory and technique remain unchanged, and will stay thus so long as men take up the bow. For instance – 'He that will come to perfection thereof, must needs begin and practise in his youth, for it is an Art, and will ask at least a full 'prenticeship', which, although referring to the desirability of starting young, applies equally to those who defer their apprenticeship a little longer; and, 'I dare be bold to affirm', continued Gervase Markham in 1634, 'that whosoever will begin, and constantly persevere, shall in the end, without question be an Archer'.

The art of archery is acquired as the result of knowledge and practice; we have attempted to present the required knowledge in this book together with guidelines as to how to set about putting into practice the principles and methods governing archery. However, no manual can guarantee results, but with a degree of patience, a moderate ability and a great deal of patience, anyone can achieve an average performance, and for those who persevere the most the rewards are the greatest.

Swalecliffe   E.G.H.
1977

1

ARCHERS FOR ALL REASONS

The reason why some people take up archery in preference to other sports cannot be easily or briefly answered. The operation of shooting an arrow from a bow is, in itself, an extremely simple act, and yet if one were to question individual archers as to the basis for their predilection for the sport, their responses would reveal a surprisingly wide variety of reasons. Whereas these reasons, on closer examination, would be relatively simple to analyse – such as the attempt by Moseley in 1801 when he said that archery attracted 'some by the novelty, some by the mode, and a few perhaps by associations of ancient chivalry and romance' – the technical aspect of shooting when it is thoroughly investigated, proves to be a matter of more complexity.

Already we have experienced some of the subtle fascination of archery by the very nature of the discussion it can provoke. Let us quickly examine some of the enthusiasm that is generated by participation in this ancient art, a pursuit which has attracted many devotees over the centuries, who would find no argument with numerous gifted authors who have written in its praise. It has been commended for many reasons; some out of practical necessity, some for political expediency and others for the sheer love of promoting the bow for the pleasures it can provide. We should, briefly, remind ourselves of earlier periods of history when the bow was a familiar and important weapon. In times of war or the threat of war, men were directed to practise with the bow by governmental decree. Usually the urgency and serious-ness of these official dictates to take up archery were barely concealed by persuasion, pointing out to the medieval conscripts that what they were doing was good for them, such as the official declaration that archery was 'an wholesome exercise for the health and strength of men'. Similar exhortations echo down the centuries – 'Join the army it will make a man of you' from the First World War is another example of skilfully contrived propaganda to get the masses to willingly carry out something or another in the national interest which otherwise would have appeared dull or pointless. Nevertheless in the fourteenth century the penalties for non-compliance of such directions were harsh; for example every able-bodied man between the ages of 15 and 60, on feast days and whenever he had leisure, was expected to learn and practise the art of shooting with bows and arrows. Those who preferred to pass their time throwing stones or indulging in football, handball, cock-fighting or 'games of no value', were imprisoned. Later such stringent methods of encouraging men to shoot in the national interest were relaxed, and a different approach was employed which met the demands of a different era. During the sixteenth century for example Bishop Latimer took up the problems of the aftermath of the Reformation, when religious and secular conditions were far from settled, and extolled archery as 'a gift of God' and a sure remedy for 'many kinds of diseases' predominant amongst which were 'glossing, gulling and whoring within the house'.

Up to this time we can identify two principal reasons for encouraging men to shoot, as a means of providing masses of ready-trained yeomen bowmen in times of war, and as an antidote for the social maladies of post-Reformation England in times of peace. Carew, writing in 1602, summarized this duality of purpose when he gave the bow a personality and made it speak out in self-praise: 'In fight I give you protection, so in peace I supply your pastime', and added the now familiar physical advantages of using the bow, 'To your limbs I yield active pliantness and to your bodies healthful exercise', a theme which has been taken up regularly ever since.

The ultimate claim for archery as a panacea was set down by William Wood in the seventeenth century:

Archers for All Reasons

It is an exercise (by proof) we see
Whose practice doth with nature best agree
Obstructions of the liver it prevents
Stretching the nerves and arteries gives extent
To the spleen's oppilations, clears the breast
And spungy lungs; it is a foe profest
To all consumptions . . .

The re-introduction of shooting with bows and arrows solely for pleasure in the eighteenth century, started a revival which has gained momentum ever since, apart from one or two setbacks mainly due to wars, and from the precepts which were laid down at that time an international brotherhood of archers has grown to embrace more than sixty nationalities. In the early years of this revival, at the turn of the nineteenth century, Thomas Roberts, a notable archer-writer, remarked: 'the tendency of archery practise is to promote and restore health and to increase and invigorate the muscular prowess of the body', and went so far as to suggest that regular use of the bow could be prescribed as a remedy against old age. In contrast with this, at about the same period, interest was stirring in the physical education of the young, and Salzmann in his book on gymnastic exercises said: 'every sport, which occupies a lad, exercises his faculties and fortifies his health, by employing him in the open air, appears to me to be of importance'.

As one of the rare outdoor occupations considered suitable for women of the leisured classes, archery was recognized as rather special. It was described, in 1793, as an art 'well becoming, ev'n in the softer sex' and, despite the somewhat reluctant concession in these words, they set a pattern for an equality of participation in the sport which was to follow. Miss Alice Legh, British Lady Champion on twenty-three occasions, extolling the virtues of archery for ladies in an article of 1894, particularly emphasized the benefits of fresh air for 'delicate and growing girls'. One must read these and many other extracts with due regard to the periods in which they were written, but the message is clear – 'I have tried archery, found pleasure from the recreation and exercise it has

5

afforded me, and I strongly recommend that you share its advantages' – an appeal closely allied to the avowed objects of the Grand National Archery Society, the national governing body for archery in the United Kingdom, which includes, 'the promotion and encouragement of archery in all its forms'.

Our hurried review of the historical encouragement of archery has indicated some of the passive advantages that the sport has to offer, now let us briefly look at the status of archery and the sort of person that is likely to be found shooting in a bow. Of course we are concerned principally with modern trends, but occasional backward glances can do no harm and, in fact, by such means the overall historical perspective of archery as a sport can be appreciated. The status of archery has changed over the centuries from being the weapon of the medieval yeoman, the soldier, the poacher and the poor man, to the plaything of nobility and a game for the rich and leisured in Georgian and Victorian times. Now, thanks to social and economic causes, archery is recognized

1. By the turn of the twentieth century archery had become a fashionable practice. Ladies' Day at the Royal Toxophilite Society in 1903.

2. The ladies' line at a tournament of the 70s, note the differences of technique and equipment compared with the earlier scene.

as a progressive international amateur sport, attracting people of both sexes from all walks of life. These changes have taken a long time to have full effect, although back in 1826, in an unpublished manuscript, H. Oldfield wrote, 'archery is an amusement that is pursued by all ranks and stations', a sentiment containing more prophecy than fact. This more universally enjoyed archery found particular popularity after each of the World Wars, which was no doubt a reaction to the war years and a welcome reversion to quieter and more leisured days.

There is no question that the exercise which is necessary for archery practice does promote physical well-being and generally tones up the body. The earlier extravagent claims have now been replaced with common-sense views as to the limitations of the bow as a cure-all, modern archers being less gullible than their earlier counterparts. The physical exertion required for a normal

7

day's shooting roughly equals that which is expended by a day's steady gardening; or put another way, you would walk about three miles or so backwards and forwards to the target and you would move the equivalent of about two and half tons during the shooting of a senior round in one day. Much less energy, in fact, than would have to be expended on some other sports.

Medical authorities have accepted archery as a most valuable aid to rehabilitation for particular classes of disability. It is taught in hospitals as a remedial exercise, particularly for those incapacitated as a result of a spinal disorder and who are confined to wheelchairs. In fact there are several clubs specifically devoted to handicapped archers and this is one of the few sports in which the disabled can compete on equal terms with the able-bodied. Recognizing this fact, archery governing bodies make special allowances in the official rules. It is interesting to note that there is a substantial psychological gain, which in itself plays an important part in the rehabilitation programme, where a disabled archer discovers that in competing against fitter opponents he can frequently achieve a higher score. Margaret Harriman, a paraplegic archer of world class, in her life story, discusses the differences between disabled and fit archers and their individual performance, and says, 'I think, however, in the final analysis, first-class shooting moves on from the physical into the mental plane, and that sitting down or standing up has very little effect on the score'. We shall return to this theme shortly.

During the last quarter of the twentieth century we have been presented with sociological studies which deplore the decline of family unity and which cite this decline as a cause of many of the social ailments from which we are suffering. In the last decade or so the variety of activities open to youth has extended considerably, sons and daughters are becoming more independent more quickly than ever before, and the opportunities to travel and to find employment far from home have increased to an exceptional degree. Attitudes have also changed and these changes have contributed to the widening gap between the generations. Despite the traumatic conditions of human society which began after the First World War and which have accelerated ever since,

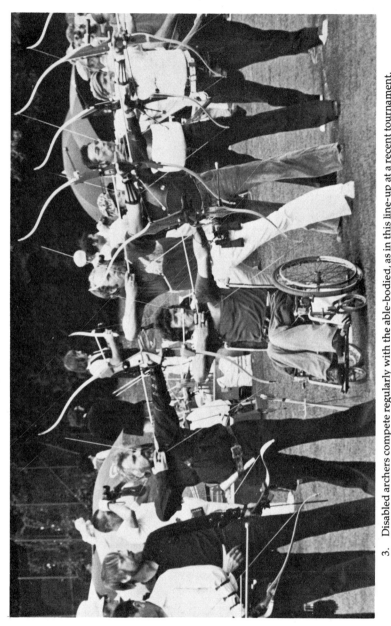

3. Disabled archers compete regularly with the able-bodied, as in this line-up at a recent tournament.

family unity is still a worth-while experience. It is difficult to think of a sport other than archery which can bring together, at one time and in one place, a family, parents and children, enjoying the same experience and even competing on equal terms with each other. That is not to say that a mixed group of, say, parents and children or old and young, both sexes, handicapped persons, even different nationalities, always join in a team experience, although this can and does often happen in tournaments, club shoots and so on. As a contrast to this group participation, another unique aspect of archery is its individuality, and the archer who likes to be alone is free to practise and compete on a highly personal basis. The sport can therefore cater for all types and is a willing slave to changing moods and specialized individual needs.

Different people approach archery in different ways, and whereas some find their pleasure in practising one type of archery, others enjoy diverse forms of shooting. There is ample choice for all inclinations, whether the urge is to endure the tough

4. Preparations for an afternoon shoot at a local club; in addition to the regular membership there is a strong junior section and an active group for beginners.

conditions of Field Archery or the measured regularity of Target Shooting, the unique precision of Flight Shooting or the convivial atmosphere of Archery Darts. Perhaps a creative ambition is waiting for release in the time-honoured occupations of bowyery and fletching, or a scholastic leaning is seeking an outlet in the study of the history of archery or in one of the many fields of research constantly being pursued by devotees of the more academic aspects of this subject. The variety of interest and the diversity of application is endless, but despite their fascination many of these ways in which bows and arrows can be enjoyed must be set aside in this book – that is apart from the practical aspects of archery. The various forms of shooting will be dealt with in turn and at length with particular emphasis on Target Archery, which is the focal point of all modern competition and the invariable starting point for all newcomers to the sport.

We have seen that archery as a sport is international, that it does not require exceptional physique to shoot in a bow, everyone is catered for, either as part of a team or as an individual, and there is no bar to age, sex or infirmity. For a moment or two let us recall a comment made by Roberts when he said that archery 'inculcates and strongly enforces a calmness and tranquility'. Let it be said at the outset that archery is no short cut to enlightenment, nor will the calmness and tranquility automatically descend when arrows are shot at a target. However, with just a little effort of mind and muscle the effects of archery will soon begin to be apparent. An increasing awareness of the usefulness of shooting a bow in an orderly fashion in producing serenity and, conversely, the usefulness of the mental processes in producing a good performance, are themes which are closely attended to by present day archers.

The theories are as yet incomplete, and possibly, as Roberts may have found and Margaret Harriman suggested over a century and a half later, the whole mysterious process defies precise description. It is rather something you feel than something which can be set down step by step in a text book. The most complete application of the more profound principles of a mental approach to shooting methods have been perfected by Zen

5. Archery is practised as a ritual way of attaining enlightenment
   by Zen Buddhists.

Buddhists in the use of archery as one of the formal disciplines or 'ways' to prepare for enlightenment. The whole process is irrational and it is a concept which cannot be grasped by formal thought, for something would have to be expressed which is inexpressible. Setting aside these metaphysical meanderings, although of great fascination and having special importance in the study of the whole process of shooting, we return to more practical terms. There is no doubt that as an antidote for the stress and strain of modern living, archery has no equal. Proof of this is simple – discover archery for yourself.

Archers are friendly folk: as a raw recruit to the sport you will find encouragement and enthusiasm from members of your local club. Advice is readily given and, what is more important, most clubs have some sort of basic training scheme in which you can join. Progress in the sport depends, quite naturally, on what you yourself want and how much time and effort you feel inclined to

6. Likely youngsters receive coaching from club instructors at regular improvement sessions.

spend on practice and learning the finer points of shooting techniques. Keen novices with the inclination can become proficient in one season, good in two, and can reach championship standard in as little as three or four seasons. Others, who want to enjoy their chosen pursuit more gently, can improve gradually over a longer period.

This book is designed to appeal to all archers, those who are new to the sport as well as those who are more experienced. The factual information we have given has been corrected up to date as far as possible and the shooting techniques which are described are a distillation of well-tried and proven methods. In recent years scores have reached levels which were considered unattainable not so long ago. This is principally due to three factors: improved equipment, more competition and better training methods. We shall present the technological background by describing the various types of equipment and how it has changed, particularly in recent years, the growth of the international competitive archery scene is outlined, and various shooting techniques are described stage by stage.

No archer has ever achieved the maximum possible score in competition, accordingly there is always room for improvement. If by reading this book and applying some of the principles outlined in it, only one archer improves as a result, then our task will have been worth-while. However, our hopes are somewhat more ambitious and, aided by the pages that follow, we trust that newcomers to the sport will begin their shooting careers with more confidence than they might have done otherwise. At the same time, for those already initiated into the intricacies of archery, there is every advantage to be gained by critical revision of individual performance and the search for improvement, and we hope that our work will provide the necessary companion for better shooting and for greater enjoyment of the sport.

PART ONE

Administration and Equipment

2

ADMINISTRATION

The usual course for anyone who decides to take up archery is to seek out a local club and become a member. This is not too difficult, as for example there are around 800 officially recognized archery clubs in the United Kingdom alone and local enquiries will soon reveal their whereabouts. Most of those clubs achieve some form of regular publicity either through local newsmedia or they may maintain permanent advertising in sports shops, in information bureaux or on notice boards in public places, canteens and social clubs. Once he is a member of a club the newcomer immediately becomes part of an organization which caters for every individual and communal need, which will include such matters as basic training, the provision of equipment, the use of a shooting ground, and numerous other amenities which we shall discuss in due course. There are other advantages in being a member of a regular club relating to competition which include the eligibility for participation in archery events and the opportunity of meeting other archers to shoot with and compete against. Without such facilities there would be little point in becoming an archer – unless of course the aim is to shoot indifferently, in unsuitable conditions, without any measure of achievement through competition.

The administration of archery is directed entirely towards participation in the sport and its enjoyment, and it follows that if the archer understands how the sport is organized and uses the system to its best advantage, then the maximum pleasure will result. There are increasing opportunities to compete on an international basis, and shooting can and does take place under national or international rules. Accordingly before the detailed practical matters relating to shooting techniques are considered it will be advantageous to look at the procedures and administration which govern the sport internationally in addition to those arrangements which apply nationally.

The organization which obtains in the United Kingdom can be regarded as a model on which other countries have based their administration, although the British example has a more complex background and a longer history than others. In the next page or so we have described the pattern in this country which can be taken as typical.

Let us begin with the now familiar local club. With a membership of maybe a dozen or so up to fifty or sixty, the majority of archery clubs are 'open', that is to say anyone is eligible for membership. In addition there are a number of 'closed' clubs which are usually sponsored by firms or organizations having their own sports or social sections which employees have the privilege of joining. Finally there are the special clubs open to certain groups in the community such as handicapped persons, young people, school-children, members of the armed services and so on. In our introductory chapter we have already briefly mentioned the importance now given to archery for the disabled and this is a subject which deserves greater space than we can allow. However perhaps the attention of one or more handicapped persons who have not yet experienced the pleasures of archery can be drawn to the sport through this book, and hopefully he or she can be encouraged to seek the many opportunities now available for its pursuit. There are, of course, problems to be overcome in matters of technique, and some adjustment of routine shooting procedures may have to be evolved with the help of qualified archery coaches. As an example of what can be achieved in this direction the Stoke Mandeville Games and the Paraplegic Olympics have no equal. In 1948 an annual archery competition was instituted at the National Spinal Centre at Stoke Mandeville and the first meeting

7.   A visitor to a local club sums up the possibility of becoming a member.

was held on the day that the Olympic Games were opened in London that year. Those taking part were all patients at the hospital or residents of the Star and Garter Homes at Richmond, who had served in the armed forces during the war. This inspiring meeting enables medically controlled paraplegics to compete in a series of sporting activities each year, and from the original sixteen competitors, the Games grew to full international status in 1952 and now takes in paraplegics from all over the world representing more than fifty countries.

It is a comforting thought that, with the help of archery, attitudes of prejudice towards the handicapped, which were formerly common, are now rapidly declining, and in recent years special encouragement and assistance in real terms has been given where it is most needed. A fine example has been set by the Worshipful Company of Fletchers who, in the last few years, have directed a substantial part of their charitable resources

19

8. This wheelchair archer has successfully overcome various technical and physical problems and is able to use standard archery tackle with commendable results.

towards helping disabled archers to acquire archery equipment, and who have given assistance to clubs for the handicapped so that the expensive items which are necessary for the pursuit of the sport can be provided. It is understood that the Company is delighted to have found a way of encouraging its ancient craft and anticipates an increase in requests for assistance as its work becomes more widely known.

As a tailpiece to these few notes concerning archery for the disabled it must be made quite clear that wheelchair archers are competitors to be reckoned with, they are not always content to shoot on their home grounds from one season to the next and they frequently take part in tournaments and competitions of all kinds. We have mentioned the Paraplegic Games, the competitors of which are all disabled, but in addition to competition exclusive to handicapped archers they can frequently be found on the shooting lines of major open meetings employing their skills on equal terms with other archers. At the 1973 World Championships at Grenoble for example, the competitors included Willie Kokott, from South Africa, shooting from a wheelchair, who put up a better score than many other perfectly fit archers, and such instances are becoming less rare as standards improve.

Archers under 18 years of age are designated as Juniors and they are specially catered for on the principle that if youngsters receive the proper training and the right encouragement, then they are more likely to continue with their archery into adulthood. Even if there is a break, whilst the more pressing attractions of growing up are dealt with, juniors can easily return to the sport as adults, because once the necessary skills have been learnt they are difficult to forget. The prowess of youthful archers cannot be ignored and some brilliant performances are now frequent events at national and international championships. In the last few years we have seen a series of teenagers taking the few top places at world events and this is clearly a trend that deserves encouragement. The Association for Archery in Schools, which was formed in 1963, is a body which attends to the needs of youthful archers by the general promotion of the

9. The junior line at a club shoot. Some of these youngsters show special promise and they take archery as seriously as their elders.

sport, arranging tournaments and so on. This association runs a summer postal league and an inter-schools team tournament held annually at the end of the season. In addition they have recently introduced the Achievement Scheme, open to juniors not only within this organization, but also to those who are members of proper affiliated archery clubs generally.

The Duke of Edinburgh's Award Scheme for boys and girls includes archery as a 'pursuit' for boys and an 'interest' for girls, and for a candidate to qualify he or she has to satisfy examiners as to his or her aptitude and enthusiasm in accordance with an official syllabus which is far from arduous or difficult. A candidate needs to be an enthusiastic archer and a trier, but not necessarily a good shot. Through this scheme, which is designed to prepare boys and girls for good citizenship, many youngsters not only learn the art of archery, but in addition, learn how to be useful club members.

Reference has already been made to 'officially recognized' and 'properly affiliated' archery clubs, and these terms should be made more clear. It is a reference to their association with the governing body for archery in the United Kingdom, the Grand National Archery Society. By this affiliation each club accepts the jurisdiction of the G.N.A.S. and conforms to the conditions, shooting rules and regulations laid down by that society. There are several classes of membership divided between individual and corporate memberships, all of whom pay an annual sub-scription or affiliation fee. The two principal qualifications for corporate membership of the society are that the clubs must also be affiliated to the regional society of the area in which they are situated and that they should be properly constituted, or in other words that there are correctly drawn up club rules which follow the accepted formula for setting up sports and social institutions.

The regional societies came into being before the national governing body for archery was instituted, and their original 'regional' character has been maintained principally by the continuance of traditional meetings in their own localities. The idea of establishing a gathering of archers from all parts of the kingdom 'as likely to improve archery, and as a social meeting to promote friendship amongst distant archers' was first suggested in 1842, and after much discussion it was finally decided to hold a meeting at York, in 1844, to be called the Grand National Archery Meeting. This meeting, which was to become the historic beginning of a series of championship meetings which still continue, was so successful that it was resolved to hold another the following year at which the ladies were to compete for the first time. In 1861 the Grand National Archery Society was formed to ensure the regular holding of annual target meetings and at the same time brought them more directly under the control of the great body of archers themselves. A set of rules was framed and the Society now had its permanent members.

Other societies of a regional nature were formed from time to time to organize championship meetings for their own areas. The Leamington and Midland Counties Meeting in 1854, the Northern Counties Archery Meeting in 1880, and in 1903 the Southern Counties Archery Meeting. In 1950, with the consent of the nine existing archery regional bodies, the G.N.A.S. was officially constituted as the national governing body to which individual clubs are affiliated. In 1977 this Society became a limited liability company. Over sixty other countries each have a similar national governing body to whom individual clubs are affiliated and it is

10. The badge of the Grand National Archery Society, the governing body for archery in the United Kingdom.

11. The emblem of the Fédération Internationale de Tir à l'Arc, the international governing body for the sport.

only fitting that as archery in its modern form has always been considered an English traditional pastime, the organizational procedures which are followed throughout the world are based on the English model.

However it is one thing to have each of a number of different countries individually organized and administered, and each looking after its own particular membership in conformity with differing environments and varying cultural requirements. It is another matter to make sense of international competitive participation by ensuring that each national body agrees to use the same set of rules and the same shooting procedures, and a standardization of these and other matters has to be agreed before any serious international events are possible. This has been achieved by the affiliation of the national associations to a world governing body, the Fédération Internationale Tir à l'Arc. The beginnings of international archery as we know it today, can be confidently assigned to the year 1931, when Poland took the initiative and held an international tournament at Lwow. It was during that year that F.I.T.A. was instituted to act as a central authority for archery with four original members, Belgium, France, Poland and Sweden. Great Britain joined the Federation the following year and since then membership has gradually grown until today there are around sixty amateur associations who are affiliated to the parent body.

The first object of F.I.T.A. is to 'promote and encourage archery throughout the world' and this is put into practice through the organization of World Championship meetings and other continental or regional championships in any branch of archery, and by framing and interpreting rules of shooting. The need to regularize rules and to standardize shooting arrangements was vital if any comparisons were to be made between the performance of archers of different nationalities. It was by following this precept that, after various changes and amendments, the current FITA Rounds were devised, and the regulations for international archery competition were laid down. The arrangements for shooting so devised have not superseded 'national' rules, particularly in so far as specific rounds are concerned, but in the last few years more interest has been taken by rank and file members of clubs throughout Britain and elsewhere in shooting international (FITA) rounds. The reason for this is clear, many of the meetings held under the auspices of most member associations are organized so that F.I.T.A. rules apply. This has several implications. For example postal matches can be conducted between clubs from different countries, in which case FITA Rounds are shot and scores exchanged by post. There is also the encouragement for individuals to enter major competitions with the extra distinction of gaining special awards and becoming eligible for selection for championship and Olympic teams.

Although the Olympic Games are somewhat outside the day to day organization of archery, in so far as it applies to individual club members, a few notes dealing with the representation of archery at the Games is of special interest, particularly in view of the untiring efforts by F.I.T.A. on behalf of archers everywhere to have archery included as an event at the Olympics.

The ultimate achievement for a competitive archer is to reach world championship standards, and the path to such heights is a steady climb through club, county, regional and national competition. The history of world championships can be related to the early participation in the Olympic Games by a relatively

12. The World Archery Championships at York in 1971.

small group of archers. Usually, as the Games moved from country to country and continent to continent, it was the archers living in the host countries who formed the majority of the competitors. For example the IVth Olympiad of 1908, held in London, saw forty British, eleven French and one lone competitor from America. It is not surprising that this situation persisted, as the inclusion of archery as an event at successive Games was achieved at the request of the national archery association of the countries where the Games were held. International rules did not exist, so the national rules of the host countries were used. In the early 1900s a series of ambitious International Archery Meetings were held at Le Touquet, and attempts were made to establish an 'international' round which would be shot at all such meetings. Although these meetings were curtailed by the First World War, the idea of an international round which could be used for competition throughout the world had been established.

It is a short step from World Championship events to the Olympics, but in the case of archery a step which has been taken in slow motion. The events which consisted of some forms of archery at the Games of 1900, 1904 and 1920 were not properly representative of international competitive archery. No universally accepted standard rules applied, and the shooting that took place was more or less a concession to the host countries who employed their own particular shooting formulas. The Games held in London in 1908 compromised to a certain extent by including both metric and imperial distances for competition, and this meeting can be considered as a positive move towards the establishment of archery as an Olympic event. Sixty-four years later, in 1972 at Munich, archery was finally included in the XXth Olympiad, with a strong international following and firmly established standardized rules of shooting.

The career of every archer is influenced by a number of factors, and one common to all is the officially published material which includes such matters as shooting regulations, safety rules and so on, which we shall deal with in more detail in the chapter that follows. As a member of a recognized club there are opportunities to participate in several schemes designed to assist archers of any proficiency in monitoring performance and equalizing standards in competition. There are also facilities to join essential programmes of training and automatic protection against claims for injury caused through the sport. Let us take the last item first. Each club in this country which is affiliated to the G.N.A.S. through a regional society, has the advantage of automatically participating in a group insurance scheme without extra payment. The cover given is in respect of damage or injury caused in the course of the sport, in any form, in the United Kingdom, but only when shooting is under the auspices of the G.N.A.S. or an affiliated body. The indemnity is on account of legal liability only and does not insure an individual in respect of personal injuries such as are covered by personal accident insurance policies. Fortunately, and due to the fact that the safety rules are properly applied, we know of no claim under this scheme; a reflection of the proper conduct of archers who are, after all, using weapons which are potentially dangerous to the point of being lethal.

The other factors that we have mentioned include the

Handicap and Classification Schemes and the coaching organization. In order that the ability of individual archers can be assessed the Handicap Scheme is used, and so that their achievements can be recognized by awards of titles appropriate to the shooting standards reached, the Classification Scheme is operated. Although optional the great majority of clubs take advantage of these official schemes, which are operated quite independantly of each other, all the administration being conducted on a club level. Both schemes have a great appeal in club archery and usually a club Records Officer is appointed who has the

13. Olympic gold medallist Darell Pace at Montreal in 1976 shooting a world breaking score.

interesting but exacting job of keeping a record of each member's scores and their subsequent gradings under both these schemes. From these records progress can be observed, success can be rewarded and accurate allowances made for use in tournaments when prizes are awarded on a handicap basis.

Before we describe the Classification and Handicap Schemes in more detail it is important to explain what is meant by a 'round'. This term has already been used and it will be met with constantly throughout your archery career. A 'round' is a set number of arrows shot at predetermined distances which vary according to the proficiency of the shooters, the type of competition, the time available and the preference of two or more archers shooting together. Traditionally rounds have always been named, and very soon the newcomer will instantly understand reference to a 'York', 'FITA' or 'Bristol' to name but three popular rounds, and a complete list of all officially recognized rounds is given on page 100.

In the Classification Scheme certain titles are awarded to archers according to their level of performance. The qualifications which are required become progressively more difficult until the exalted rank of Grand Master Bowman is reached, but although relatively few archers achieve this exacting standard there is ample scope in the lesser ranks of Master Bowman, and Class I, II, or III Archers. This scheme is operated quite simply; to gain Class I, II, or III an archer must shoot during the calendar year, three rounds of, or better than, the scores set out in the table below. These qualifying rounds must be shot at a Club Target Day [see G.N.A.S. Rule 150] or at a meeting organized by G.N.A.S. or by a body affiliated to it and under G.N.A.S. Rules of Shooting, where a minimum of two archers are shooting together. Immediately the requisite scores are made, the upgrading occurs, but if during a second year the archer is unable to make the necessary scores in his class, then he is relegated to a class below on January 1st of the third year. The titles of Grand Master Bowman and Master Bowman are more difficult to obtain, the standard of the former has been made very high indeed and qualifications can only be gained at major tournaments, whereas,

14. A 10-year old practises the finer points of technique under the guidance of his father who has qualified as an Instructor.

although the standard of Master Bowman is high, only half the qualifying rounds have to be shot at major meetings.

There is a modified Classification Scheme for junior archers for which the titles of Master Bowman and Class I, II and III Archers are awarded, and although the rounds and qualifying scores differ, all the other arrangements are the same as those which apply to seniors.

Precise instructions for operating the Handicap Scheme are included in the set of Handicap Tables issued by the G.N.A.S. The principle by which this scheme works is that the score of any given round has a corresponding handicap figure, based on the presumption that a score of 800 for a York Round equals zero or scratch. Scratch scores for each of twelve rounds have been assessed and handicap figures ranging from 60 to minus 40 are matched by their corresponding scores. Thus any archer, whether he be average or expert, shooting a standard round, can easily find the handicap equivalent for his score. This figure is

31

Qualifying scores for the Classification Scheme

GENTLEMEN

	York	FITA	St. George	New Western	New National	Long Metric	Short Metric	Hereford	Albion	Long Western	Long National	Western	National	Windsor	American
G.M.B.	1000	1220													
M.B.		1150													
1st Class	800	980	644	515	370	434	481	806	642	526	378	521	382	629	524
2nd Class	620	820	516	391	276	339	404	633	517	410	289				
3rd Class	450	650	388	275	191	245									

LADIES

	Hereford	FITA	Albion	Long Western	Long National	Long Metric	Short Metric	Western	National	Windsor	American
G.M.B.	1000	1200									
M.B.		1100									
1st Class	800	895	639	522	374	421	384	523	382	635	529
2nd Class	620	710	511	400	279	324	297	406	294	510	425
3rd Class	450	530	383	286	195	232					

reduced as the archer's performance improves, according to a straightforward set of rules which are easy to assimilate and simple to apply.

A handicap figure provides the individual archer with a ready means of making comparisons of his scores over a season which would otherwise be well-nigh impossible. Included in the official handicap publication are useful tables showing the score anticipated for each dozen arrows shot at different distances according to a specific handicap figure. With a handicap figure available, an allowance can be calculated and allocated to an archer so that he can compete on an equal basis against archers of a higher or lower standard. It will be apparent that the lower the standard of the archer, the greater will be his handicap allowance. Many tournaments and club fixtures include awards based on handicapped scores, which means that the individual is neither penalized by being a poor shot nor would he have a special advantage by being an expert.

Every archer at one time or another needs extra help with his shooting and encouragement to better his own performance. The G.N.A.S. Coaching Scheme was originally devised to cope with the post-war expansion of archery, and now it caters for those archers who wish to train as coaches progressively for club, county and region. To co-ordinate these activities a number of coaching organizers are appointed. The services of archery coaches, which are quite voluntary, are normally available on request, and instruction is given at the club's own ground usually to groups of archers, in addition to which short courses of a day or weekend are arranged regularly at convenient locations so that a greater number of archers can participate. If a club has amongst its members an archer keen enough to become a club coach then, of course, instructing new members or brushing up the performance of those already shooting, presents no problems.

The National Coaching Organization sets a number of progressive examinations, and archers who seek coaching status must first qualify as instructors. This provides the necessary training for teaching beginners in clubs. After a two-year period an instructor can then qualify as a County Coach when his activities

33

are widened under the direction of a County Coaching Organizer. A County Coach who serves for a further three years, and after taking the appropriate examination, can then become elevated to Regional Coach, and when he or she has operated on this level for a further three years he or she may be selected to become a Senior Coach. By this system the sport is assured of a group of dedicated coaches who have had wide experience and who are able to provide a first-class voluntary service for training archers at all levels.

In the following chapter we will examine the way in which archery is pursued, by discussing the general procedures for shooting, reviewing the rules which are common to all archers and outlining some idea of what to expect and what is expected on the archery field.

3

THE RULES

In this chapter it is our intention to provide a review of the rules and regulations which form the basis for modern archery practice, and, what is important, where they are to be found, together with some general notes on the traditional usages which are currently practised. The rules which we deal with are primarily designed for Target Archery, and as this particular form of shooting is dealt with fully from a practical aspect in later chapters we will mention detailed aspects of the rules as they become appropriate throughout the book. The official rules include separate regulations for a number of different forms of shooting which include Target Archery, both indoor and outdoor, Field Archery, Flight Shooting, Clout Shooting, Archery Golf, Archery Darts and Popinjay Shooting. Also included are the official arrangements which are required for national tournaments, regulations for junior archery and details of qualifications and awards for the schemes we mentioned in the previous chapter. In later chapters we will briefly discuss the various alternative forms of shooting which can be practised together with quotes from the rules when they are applicable.

In Target Archery a round, which as we have seen consists of a specified number of arrows shot at predetermined distances, must be completed before scores can be recorded. When any round is shot, each archer, after shooting six arrows as non-scoring sighters, shoots three arrows and then retires until all the other archers shooting at the same target have also shot three. A repetition of this process marks the completion of an 'end' of six arrows. Scores are then taken, the arrows withdrawn from the target, and the next end shot. Further ends are shot in this fashion until the total number of arrows in the round have been discharged. This, in simple terms, is how a round – the basis of all formalized Target Archery – is shot. However, it is important to remember that shooting has to be carefully controlled, and a number of special circumstances can arise which may call for the application of previously agreed rules. In addition it is essential that all archers should experience the same conditions in competition. Accordingly there are three basic factors which determine the necessity for having rules: ensuring the safety of competitors and spectators, for a thoughtless shot may be a fatal one; a standard procedure before, during and after shooting which allows for all eventualities and prevents disputes; and the control of conditions which are common to all competitors.

Despite the fairness in all the shooting rules and the scrupulous manner with which archers adhere to them, it has been known, very rarely we hasten to add, that falsification of scores has taken place. This is a strange phenomenon, for in this particular sport the gain is nil, and the only person being cheated is the cheater. But enough of that disagreeable subject which has demonstrated the fact that no set of rules is infallible, and it is hardly necessary to add that the only way such rules can operate satisfactorily is by fair play and the total co-operation of those who agree to accept them.

Let us examine more closely the rules of shooting which have evolved over many years and which have resulted from careful study of what is needful to make the art of archery an enjoyable and satisfying pursuit. It is really nothing more than the application of simple, common sense procedures. The regulations for shooting which must be adhered to by members of all clubs affiliated to the G.N.A.S., are contained in *Rules of Shooting* published by that body as a pocket-sized volume which is amended from time to time. It is at least desirable that every archer should provide himself with a copy of this publication and, what is more important, he should ensure that it is kept up

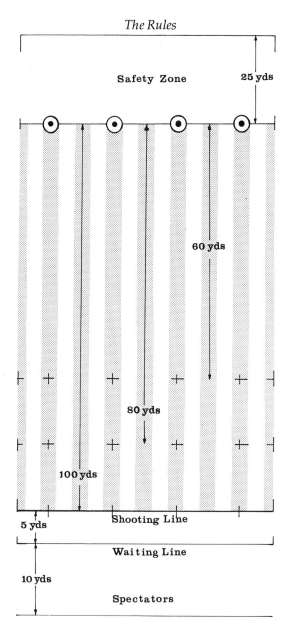

Safety Zone   25 yds

60 yds

80 yds

100 yds

5 yds   Shooting Line

Waiting Line

10 yds

Spectators

15. A typical layout for an archery meeting in which the shooting line moves forward to accommodate the lesser distances as the round progresses.

37

16. The William Somner Tournament in progress in which the shooting line and the waiting line can be clearly seen.

to date. The extracts that we have quoted throughout this book have been taken from the 1977 edition.

After the newcomer to archery has learnt the basic method of shooting and can, with some confidence, discharge arrows in the general direction of the target, he will be anxious to progress by the shooting of a round. Nonetheless whilst in the early stages of his archery career he will have been instructed on a few essential matters which apply no matter whether basic training is taking place or a competitive round is being shot.

We begin by reviewing those rules which directly apply to the safety of archers and others who may not be shooting. Many of these rules particularly apply to organized meetings, but the principles they embody are equally valid for club shooting and they should be interpreted accordingly. Firstly, all shooting should take place at an archery field officially recognized as such. The indiscriminate use of gardens, parks, common land or public places, no matter how safe they may appear, is contrary to the official regulations, and any archery practice which takes place under such arrangements would not be recognized either for insurance purposes or in connection with the recording of scores under the various schemes approved by G.N.A.S. The direction in this matter is clear: to be affiliated to the parent body a club must be properly constituted, this process involves a written constitution which includes a definition of the club's shooting ground which is duly registered as such.

Then there are the logical requirements to make that ground safe, for example a sparse hedge next to a busy thoroughfare is insufficient protection against, for instance, sudden incursions of small boys, curious about the activity but innocent of the danger lurking in the sudden flash of a badly loosed arrow.

Each archer must have complete mastery over every shot, and to aim indiscriminately without knowing where the arrow will land is a thoughtless and unforgivable practice. Unnecessary risks can be disconcerting to other archers and this in turn can lead to bad shooting, the archer's attention having been distracted and he becomes worried by potential dangers. Thus it is logical to assume that by the elimination of practices which are dangerous, the way is cleared for uninterrupted concentration on good shooting, apart from dispelling potential danger, and a simple but effective rule which is emphasised from the very start of shooting, is that which reads: *A bow may not be drawn except on the shooting line and in the direction of the target.* [Rule 105 (p)]. It is also important to exercise complete control over the movements of everyone on the archery field, no matter whether they are taking part in the shooting, or are there as spectators or visitors, and the rules are quite clear on this point. *Archers, other than those actually shooting or moving to or from the shooting line, shall remain behind the waiting line.* [Rule 105 (q)] *On grounds where the public have access an area shall be roped off to ensure that no one can pass behind the targets within 25 yards of them and that no one can approach within 10 yards of the ends of the shooting line* [Rule 101 (i)]. A signal is given for the commencement of shooting and this practice is invariably followed whenever shooting takes place, at club shoots or at tournaments, and the rule reads: *The Judge or Field Captain shall sound the whistle for assembly 15 minutes before the time appointed for shooting, and shall sound it again as the signal to start shooting. The Judge shall indicate when each end is completed, and no archer shall advance from the shooting line before receiving the signal.* [Rule 105 (d)]. At an organized meeting the only practice allowed on the shooting ground is one end of six arrows which may be shot as 'sighters'. These sighters are invariably shot at the commencement of any round and they do not score nor are they recorded in any way. [Rule 104 (k)]. The value of these sighters in adjusting bow sights and assisting the archer to settle down in shooting will become more apparent when we discuss such matters in later chapters.

We have given extracts of some rules in detail as they govern the general pattern of movement on an archery field. There are some variations depending on the particular meeting, as for example the method of signalling at major championships, World Championships and the Olympics, but the overall principles remain unchanged. There is a warning cry which should be used by an archer if he sees some good reason why shooting should stop, and this shout of 'FAST' is immediately recognized and obeyed. Alternatively several blasts on a whistle is the recognized danger signal. It is interesting to note that safety regulations can claim an ancient ancestry. During the reign of Henry VIII, for instance, a law was made absolving archers from any responsibility if they accidentally injured or killed a passer-by, provided they were shooting at recognized butts and so long as they cried 'FAST' as a warning that shooting was in progress.

In addition to the safety rules and the regulations controlling movement on the archery field, the actual routine of shooting has to be covered by proper rules, and this important aspect is under the control of an official, the Judge or Field Captain if it is a tournament, or a member appointed to attend to such matters if it is a club shoot. The whole of Rule 105 deals with the control of shooting under these officials, whose authority, as we have already seen, extends to other matters requiring decisions connected with the meeting. Accordingly it is most desirable that

17. Most tournaments award a prize for the best gold of the day and here the Judge is measuring a qualifying shot.

the Judge, who may delegate certain duties to a Field Captain, [Rule 105 (n) & (o)] must have a wide experience of archery in general and shooting procedures in particular, he must be able to exercise tact in contentious matters, and above all be able by positive direction to ensure that the archery meeting over which he presides proceeds smoothly and as efficiently as possible. It can be seen how important the training of such paragons must be, and this is one of the vital roles carried out by the Coaching Organization, who provide, by their programmes of training and examination, suitable persons willing and able to act as Judges at tournaments and meetings, not only in this country but also on an international basis.

Archery meetings of the past were graced by a lady patroness

41

who generally presided over the meeting and in particular dispensed a collection of quite valuable prizes; very often this lady was hostess for the day, as more often than not the shooting took place in the grounds of her country home. Long before this each contestant at a medieval tournament would be favoured by the patronage of a lady to inspire him to greater feats of arms. It appears that the lady for whom the highest ranking knight fought became the Lady Paramount, but her actual duties, apart from being a decoration and an inspiration, are not altogether clear. Somewhere along the passage of time the archery patroness took the earlier title of her medieval ancestor and nowadays we have presiding at all our archery meetings a Lady Paramount. This is no casual office, nor is it one which is purely decorative, and Rule 105 (a) defines this appointment precisely: *The Lady Paramount shall be the supreme arbitrator on all matters connected with the tournament at which she officiates.* This is another instance of an aspect of tradition being firmly implanted in the formal regulations which control the sport, but there are other matters which, although distinguished by long standing habit, are not strictly enforceable. They are, however, invariably followed by all those who shoot under G.N.A.S. rules. It is significant that part of the Society's motto reads: 'Union, True Heart and Courtesy', because the so-called unwritten rules of etiquette are not only a display of good manners, they also indicate a general agreement amongst archers that the observance of some simple matters can assist in the smooth running of any meeting, and what is more they can help good shooting – a very practical advantage. They are worth repeating.

Whilst shooting is in progress it is discourteous for any archer on the shooting line or elsewhere on the field to talk in a loud voice to the annoyance of others. It can be quite distracting to a person concentrating on shooting, particularly at the critical moment before the 'loose', to be disturbed by a sudden noise of any kind, and a thoughtless exclamation can, and often does, ruin what otherwise would have been a good shot. Observers of human behaviour are unanimous in their assessment of a group of archers as being congenial and of one accord. But there are

18. When calling the score values of shots each archer must point to but not touch the arrows scored.

special moments when the individual, be he novice or champion, cogitates over some particular personal problem of shooting and at such moments resists the attempts of others to converse. It is then bad sportsmanship to talk to him if he obviously prefers to remain silent.

Although the Judge or Field Captain is responsible for the timing of shooting and the movement of archers to and from the shooting line and the targets, he is unable to officiate over the unrestricted movements of archers when they are not actually shooting. Scores are normally recorded on sheets which are attached to boards for ease in handling, and in their competitive zest some archers stalk up and down behind the shooting line studying other archers' scores and comparing them with their own. The official who controls shooting has no power to prevent this, which is nevertheless considered very bad manners. A group of archers is allocated to one target and one of these is designated as Target Captain to record the scores of his target mates. This is an unenviable task and few relish the extra work, but nevertheless this is part of the whole procedure of archery and the job is invariably performed willingly and cheerfully. To facilitate this work it is expected that scores will be called in a regular fashion to save confusion. Six arrows have to be accounted for and the recommended method of calling the scores is to call them in groups of three, the highest first, and the value of each arrow is called separately – even those that do not score! For example: 'nine – seven – seven', pause, 'five – three – zero'. The Target Captain is customarily thanked for his work at the end of each round.

Some archers pay considerable sums of money for their tackle, other provide for themselves very economically, but whatever their value these possessions are highly prized by their owners, and a good archer cares for his equipment like a mother for her child. It is extremely bad manners to touch another's equipment without first seeking the owner's permission. Accidents can happen however, and if any archer breaks another's arrow for instance, through his own carelessness, he pays for it on the spot.

The G.N.A.S. *Rules of Shooting* contain several polite reminders of tradition, pointing out what is expected of archers in certain situations, rather than forcefully declaring that such matters are inflexible rules. For example: *Any archer who has won one or more of the Society's medals is expected to wear one at least at every subsequent Championship or Handicap Meeting at which he or she shall compete.* There are few sports which do not have an accepted form of dress or turnout, and whereas today there is a wider display of individual preference for style of dress than a generation or so ago, the majority of archers make a special effort to dress in a manner which is both practical and in accordance with customary usage. The traditional colour for archery is green, and the habit of wearing this colour can be traced back over the centuries. At one time the Grand National Archery Society attempted to bring in a rule for dress of a standard green, which was to be worn by all members of clubs and societies in the United Kingdom, but this was strongly opposed and finally rejected. Contemporary rules

19. Provided that the competitive archer dresses within the rules there is no reason why comfort should be ignored.

20. Many women find that slacks are the most practical form of dress for the archery field.

do contain dress regulations, but these are for three specific meetings, the Grand National Archery Meeting, the National Championship Meeting and the International Trial. However there is a note appended to the dress regulations which reads: *The accepted dress should be encouraged whenever organized shooting takes place including Club Target Days.* A situation which is far more acceptable than the previous attempts to compel the wearing of

21. There are no restrictions as to skirt lengths, as can be seen from this and the following picture, and archers are free to dress in accordance with their own preference.

22. Different texture and designs retaining the desired overall effect of dark green and white.

standard dress. The accepted dress (Appendix E) consists of trousers, shirt and/or sweater for gentlemen, and dress, skirt and blouse or trousers and blouse plus a sweater or cardigan as required for ladies. Each garment may be plain dark green or plain white and there is no objection to wearing green and white garments together. The British Council specification for the recommended colour is either Bottle Green No. 25, Tartan Green No. 26, or Rifle Green No. 27.

A Club Target Day, which has already been mentioned, has been defined by Rule 150, summarized as follows – a Club Target Day should be included in a pre-arranged programme of club events, the number of which being unlimited, arranged throughout the season. On these days there must be a minimum of two archers shooting, not necessarily on the same target, and scores on that day must be recorded. It means therefore that, although there is no restriction on casually arranged shoots, the scores made on such days would not be recognized for record or award purposes, and it is therefore important that regular advance planning of club fixtures should be carried out.

Some outline has already been given of the part played by the Fédération Internationale de Tir à l'Arc (F.I.T.A.) in the organization of international competition, and for these purposes *Constitution and Rules* is published by that body which supplement rather than replace national rules. There are some modifications specifically designed for higher standards of control of tournaments, which are requirements under international regulations. Whereas these rules have to be applied when F.I.T.A. Rounds are shot at specific major tournaments, they can be applied optionally by the organizers of tournaments which do not have this international status. The relevant rules have been extracted and are set out for easy reference in Appendix K to G.N.A.S. *Rules of Shooting*.

The eligibility code of the International Olympic Committee spells out the danger of creating pseudo-amateurs by subsidizing individuals because of their athletic ability, by governments, educational institutions, or business concerns. It also points out that inducements of various kinds offered solely to create national aggrandisment, advertising promotions, and prestige, conflict with the principles of amateurism, and therefore do not accord with the spirit and aims of the Olympic movement. This has certain implications in so far as archery is concerned, as for example, in recent years various traditional sweepstakes at archery meetings have been dropped to avoid contravention of Olympic regulations, and thus the possibility of individuals becoming ineligible for Olympic competition has been avoided.

Wagers, lotteries and sweepstakes were once accepted as part of the customary proceedings at most archery meetings. For example the traditional 'gold sweep', which until recently was an invariable feature of major tournaments, invited competitors to pay an equal share at the commencement of shooting and, according to the number of 'golds', or central shots, scored that day, they were paid out proportionately. Another custom was the payment of a pre-decimal shilling by all competitors shooting the same round to the archer who scored six consecutive golds – known as a 'perfect end'. Nowadays the official recognition of this achievement is the award of a Six-gold Badge, which has to be gained at distances of at least sixty yards for ladies and eighty yards for gentlemen, or at the seventy and sixty metres and ninety and seventy metres distances respectively. (Rule 290).

It is hoped that from the above notes anyone taking up the bow for the first time will have the satisfaction of knowing that the support of a highly organized and efficient international federation reaches even the smallest club, and what is possibly even more important is the knowledge that the national organization of every country, having membership of the World Federation, is particularly geared to encourage newcomers to the sport, in addition to constant endeavours by each of these bodies to improve facilities for archers of all standards.

4

EQUIPMENT

One aspect of archery which has a particular appeal for many of its followers is its individuality. When we discuss the shooting techniques and methods by which the sport is pursued, this unique quality will become more apparent, and once the newcomer becomes confident and progresses to serious shooting a realization of this uniqueness will undoubtedly follow and will play an important part in the archer's career. The best archers are those who seek to improve their own performance, it is a very individual challenge and one which requires personal discipline. If any progress is to be made in the sport the archer first has to be absolutely confident in the bows and arrows he is using, and he has to satisfy himself that they are the best possible choice for him and for him alone. Without this confidence the beginner, and the more experienced too, will tend to blame his equipment if progress lags. Conversely it is pointless and frustrating trying to improve if the faults lie in the equipment and not the archer, and all too often aspiring beginners, disheartened by an apparent inability to improve, have given up archery altogether, whereas by guidance as to the critical matters of choosing equipment at the start, they would have had the chance of experiencing the pleasure of shooting well.

The primary factor which determines the selection of bows and arrows is the physique of the archer, involving a number of criteria which govern the correct weight of the bow and the length of arrows, such as the fact that an archer must be capable

23. A familiar topic of discussion at any archery meeting involves archery tackle and its performance.

of comfortably drawing his bow back to its fullest extent a certain number of times during a day's shooting, and that the arrows he is using must be neither too long nor too short for him or for the bow. Added to that the equipment must be capable of carrying out the task prescribed for it by the owner. Once these basic matters are resolved, which have depended entirely on the stature and strength of the archer, a secondary factor, a mental acceptance and a satisfaction that all is in order, can then be realized and the way is clear for concentration on the actual techniques of shooting. Therefore a careful initial study of the equipment that is available can only be advantageous, that is if archery is to be approached in a deliberate and thorough fashion. After all, if one is taking up the sport, or has already investigated its possibilities, why not take advantage of everything it offers?

One inevitable topic of discussion amongst archers concerns the bows and arrows they use; whether they be novices who have recently taken up the sport or experts who have reached international standards, whenever they meet they will discuss the relative merits of one type of bow compared with others, the intricacies of design, performance, and the many details of the great variety of tackle that is now available. The finer technical points may bewilder the uninitiated, but the basic fact which prompts such discussion is, in brief, the search for the best equipment for the individual.

Not so long ago bows and arrows were generally produced commercially in two sizes, one for men and the other for ladies. If you happened to be the right size for the equipment you had a reasonable chance of making a success of archery, otherwise very soon you took up an alternative sport. Archery manufacturers in the last few decades, however, have become more enlightened, and bows and arrows are now readily available in a bewildering range of specifications to suit anyone, including the most exacting customer. There is, of course, a limit to exclusiveness, but what is important for the individual at the outset is for him, or her, to make a considered selection of the most suitable equipment, and this choice, as we have suggested, should be made with one or two simple facts in mind.

The choice of a bow should be governed by the size and general physique of the archer. All bows are measured by the weight in pounds avoirdupois that have to be exerted to draw arrows of specified lengths. This is not so complicated as it sounds. For example a bow may be listed as drawing 35 pounds at 28 inches, although shorter arrows could be used in the same bow, in which case they would require less poundage to draw them fully. Under no circumstances should arrows which are longer than the prescribed length be used in a bow, particularly for reasons of safety. The choice of the weight of the bow is critical, because using a bow that is too strong to be comfortably handled, that is by being 'overbowed', will prove disastrous in trying to develop a good performance. On the other hand to be 'underbowed' can be frustrating, for although each arrow can be drawn with effort to spare, it will soon be found that when the time comes to progress to greater distances the bow is just not capable of projecting the arrow to the target, other than by an excessively high trajectory which, in turn, can be a handicap to accurate shooting. An archer should use the strongest bow he can handle without undue fatigue in a full day's shoot, the important point being that the bow must still be under the same control at the end of the day as it was when shooting began. It is therefore wise to make a careful choice of bow weight, and in making that choice it is best to seek advice from a qualified club instructor or coach, and above all do not be in too much of a hurry to make a decision because the right equipment is the basis for all good shooting.

Arrows, too, have to be chosen with care and their selection depends on the understanding of some vital statistics. Arrows are supplied in sets of eight, six to be used in normal shooting and two reserved as spares, although any number can usually be purchased if required. They are made to a series of specifications which include weight, length and 'spine' which relates to the stiffness, springiness or vibration period factor. Spine is measured by the amount of bending which occurs in a controlled application of weights, and is recorded in G.N.A.S. units as a spine rating. The science of ballistics explains why the maximum efficiency can be obtained from a projected arrow which has its stiffness matched to the power of the released bow-string combined with its mass. Therefore arrows can only be correctly selected if the specification of the bow from which they are to be shot is known, and the primary considerations for such selection are weight and spine. Fortunately most arrow manufacturers publish useful tables giving concise information as to the specifications of arrows.

The length of arrows is determined entirely by the physical measurements of the archer. Although a novice can shoot well enough with arrows a little too long for him to begin with, once he has become more proficient the arrow length must be carefully selected to suit his particular physique. A rough initial guide as to a suitable arrow length can be ascertained by holding an arrow between the hands held together at arms' length extended in front of the body, with the butt end of the arrow placed high on the breast bone. A more accurate measurement of the correct length can be achieved by enrolling the help of an observer who

24. A simple method of ascertaining the length of arrows required by a beginner.

can measure the exact length of an arrow held at full draw in the bow. The size, weight, shape and balance of an arrow will chiefly influence the distance to which it will fly, but spine with straightness will decide whether it will go in the direction in which it is aimed.

An arrow with its spine matched to the speed with which it passes the bow will not actually touch the bow at all from the moment the string is loosed. In the operation of a simple bow, although the released string returns to rest in direct line with the central axis of the bow limbs, the arrow changes its line of direction in a manner quite considerably due to the thickness of the bow limb deflecting it from a direct line before the string has completed its journey. The initial impact of the released string on the arrow actually bends it towards and then away from the side of the bow, 'A' and this oscillation continues during the time the string is pushing forward. Finally, if the oscillation period is just right, the tail end of the arrow curves round the bow, its fletching nicely clearing all obstacles 'B'. Once clear of the bow and free of the string the arrow rights itself by springing back to bend in the reverse plane and continues a series of diminished oscillations until it is flying on its original and intended course 'C'. The resistance to bending, or degree of suppleness, recorded as we have said in units of spine, is therefore of paramount importance. This strange behaviour of an arrow as it leaves a bow has been

25. The Archer's Paradox as viewed from above.

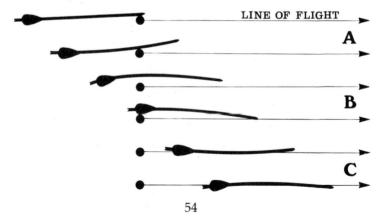

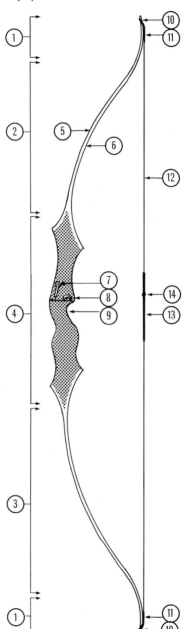

26. Parts of a bow.
    1. Recurves
    2. Upper limb
    3. Lower limb
    4. Handle riser
    5. Back of bow
    6. Belly of bow
    7. Clicker
    8. Arrow-rest
    9. Hand-grip
    10. Nocks
    11. Loop servings
    12. Bowstring
    13. Centre serving
    14. Nocking point

called the Archer's Paradox, and it is a problem which has been studied rather more than other archery phenomenom. Experiments and research have added to our knowledge of arrow flight and have contributed greatly to bow and arrow design. The problems of the Archer's Paradox begin to fade if the width of the bow at the point where the arrow leaves it, is reduced, the advantage being that the amount of oscillation required to clear

27.   The traditional English longbow.

the bow is reduced and consequently the matching of arrows to a bow becomes simplified.

References have been made to the technological advances which have been made to bow design over the past forty years, developments which are probably unique in sports history, and which have made a major contribution to the popularity of the sport. A transformation in design occurred with bewildering speed during the period following the Second World War. A detailed account of these developments are available elsewhere and our brief outline of the principal changes should be sufficient for all but the engineer or scientist.

The bow that was used for centuries by target archers, and which has been responsible for countless arrows thudding into targets, to say nothing of those that found their marks much earlier in the enemies of England, was the traditional longbow, usually made of yew, but often produced in other, less exotic, but almost as efficient, woods to satisfy a demand for cheaper bows. An interesting sidelight on this subject is the fact that these cheaper bows were often stained to represent yew, no doubt as a matter of prestige and to avoid appearing on the shooting line as a poor relation.

Prior to the Second World War, around 1935, a tubular steel bow made its first appearance on the shooting lines in Britain and in the United States as somewhat of a novelty. But when scores were compared it was soon apparent that this product of precision engineering was responsible for greater accuracy and therefore better performances from individuals than was possible with the traditional longbow. The pioneers of this revolutionary advance were a Swedish firm, and as demand grew for this new form of bow, British manufacturers soon took up the challenge and established departments to design, produce and market these bows. The decline of the steel bow, which in its turn had ousted the longbow, was marked by the introduction to archers of the modern composite bow in the mid-1960s.

The history of the evolution of the composite bow is longer than most archers realize, for it was in the seventeenth century, when difficulties were experienced in obtaining supplies of

28.   A group of simple composite bows.

foreign yew, that bowyers were induced to 'back' inferior yew staves with hickory, ash or elm, thus anticipating a development that would transform bow design two or three centuries later. Although strictly speaking not 'composite' in form, this principle of using laminated materials with differing qualities to improve bow performance can be likened to the method of bow construction which had been used for many hundreds of years previously by Asiatic bowyers who employed horn and animal sinew to make their weapons. The habit of backing bows became commonplace, and the use of materials other than wood for this purpose was not unknown nearly two centuries ago. For example an advertisement of 1793 reads: *A bow backed with whalebone will prevent it from breaking,* and this would have no doubt also somewhat improved the performance of the bow. Research and development during and after the 1939-45 War produced plastics with excellent characteristics for reliably storing and releasing energy through stress loading and unloading. Applications of these new materials were soon perfected and the horn and sinew of the old form of composite bow have now been replaced by strong plastics with fibre-glass reinforcements.

The modern composite bow has limbs rectangular in section, with adequate width to ensure stability against twisting as the

29.   A modern composite bow with detachable limbs.

bow is drawn. The design is aimed at employing the whole limb, including the backwardly curved ends, for storing energy, and each limb 'works' throughout with approximately the same stored energy in each unit of volume of the stressed limbs. The limbs are built up on a thin inner core of wood, usually hard maple, to both sides of which specially developed plastic laminations are bonded. Several manufacturers have introduced

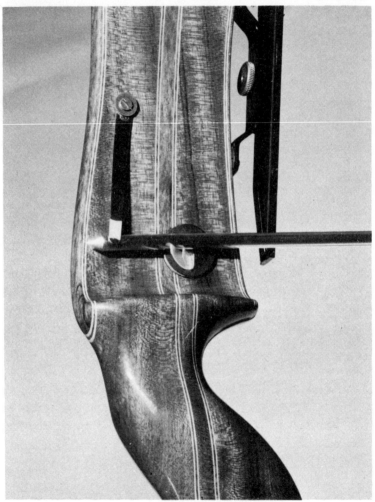

30. A typical sculptured hand-grip. Also shown is the arrow in position under the clicker and resting on the arrow-rest.

take-apart composite bows in recent years, which generally consist of a centre handle section of lightweight magnesium to which bow limbs are locked and bolted. The advantages of this type of bow are portability, and the ease with which the limbs can be inter-changed or replaced according to the archer's needs.

A comparison between supplier's catalogues of today and those of say twenty five years ago, will reveal the introduction of many new features of design, special devices, and aids to good

31.   Examples of various types of stabilizer systems.

shooting. Prominent amongst these are the now standard sculptured hand grips, which have been designed to ensure that the force applied by the bow hand has a constant location; the clicker, a lightweight spring fixed to the side of the bow, under which the arrow is drawn and which gives an audible signal when the correct draw length is achieved; and stabilizer systems, possibly the most spectacular items of gadgetry yet introduced, with a proliferation of counter-balance weights, antennae, angle brackets, knobs and adjusters. There are so many extra arrangements available in these systems, which are designed to compensate torque, or twisting of the bow when release takes place, that they have been limited to four per bow by Rule 103 (g). The merits of such appurtenances in providing the archer with the means to make better scores can only be proved by individual experience, and our advice to newcomers to archery is to first become reasonably proficient with less complex equipment, before embarking on the more elaborate, and more expensive, tackle. Then, and then alone, will you be able to judge the worth of these advanced applications of bow design.

There is no question that the modern composite bow has proved to be the most efficient yet developed; it is safe, it has relative immunity to normal temperature and humidity variations, and over a long day's shooting its performance is unchanged. Whereas the longbow was notoriously subject to variation in its performance according to changes in temperature or humidity, its mechanical efficiency was much less than that of composite bows, and it was liable to break if not properly cared for. The steel bow did not possess all these disadvantages, but it too was somewhat unstable in that it had a nasty habit of shattering at full draw due to metal fatigue, which encouraged the general wearing of peaked caps as some protection from facial bruising or worse.

The latest, and somewhat controversial, bow which has been devised is what is called a 'compound' bow. The limbs and centre section are similar in construction to the regular composite bow, but there the similarity ends. The design is based on the principle of assisted energy storing through a system of pulleys over which runs the bow string. The manufacturers of these bows claim faster arrow flight and accordingly a flatter trajectory, therefore requiring a smaller amount of sight adjustment. There is also the added advantage of less interference from wind and air currents. Just how much can be added to a bow before it becomes transformed into a purely mechanical device is a question of profound importance, and this is a problem which has received considerable attention during the past decade or so, with

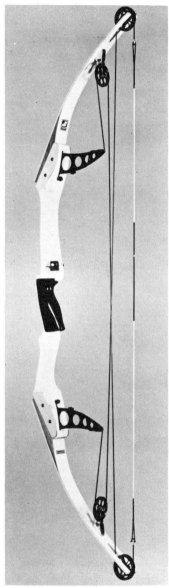

particular regard to the compound bow. Various mechanical or other release aids are not permitted by Rule 103 (i), and the authorities have ruled that bows which *incorporate any device to secure a mechanical advantage by means of cams, pulleys, levers or any similar arrangements* and which do not meet the requirements of F.I.T.A. Rules of Shooting, are not recognized. [Rule 102 (b)]. However such bows may be used in shooting G.N.A.S. rounds provided they are not used in direct competition with other more conventional bows, and that scores made with compound bows are not submitted in connection with claims for awards or for classifications.

There is clearly an implication that the performance of these bows is superior, and there is a probability that it will be felt necessary to set up a separate class for users of compound bows. For traditionalists, though, these new-fangled weapons will remain outside what is considered to be 'proper' archery.

32. The complexities of the compound bow.

A form of bow which has proved very popular in recent years, and which has developed from the technological advances in man-made materials, is constructed of solid fibre-glass. These bows are virtually indestructible, they are excellent bows for beginners and they are very reasonably priced. However despite their modest appearance and cost they are perfectly capable of a good consistent performance, and they are particularly recommended as practice bows. Other detailed features of modern bows will be mentioned in due course when particular technical aspects of shooting are discussed.

The modern arrow is a missile of great refinement, and its simple appearance does little to advertise the fact that a great amount of research has been devoted to its improvement. At one time all arrows were made from wood, difficult to match in weight and suppleness, unreliable in so far as straightness was

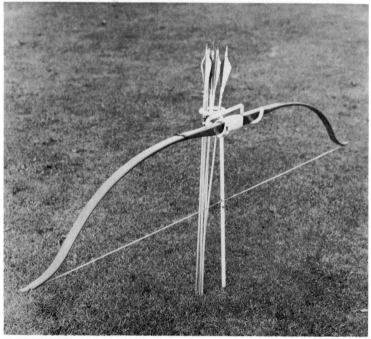

33. A fibre-glass bow, note the use of the ground quiver.

concerned, notoriously subject to splintering on impact and temperamental in performance. Nowadays the greatest majority of arrows used are made from high tensile alloy tube, precision drawn, with constant physical properties such as stiffness and mass per unit length for each diameter and wall thickness. A matched set of modern target arrows have a guaranteed tolerance of weight of as little as one grain between them. Another variable factor, that of drag, has been reduced by replacing natural feathers with vanes of plastic. Arrow shafts made from tubes of fibre-glass have found popularity with some archers; they are robust and do not bend and they can be used as an alternative to alloy arrows with equal success.

The basic equipment of an archer includes two accessories which are essential, and without which good shooting would be that much more difficult to achieve. They are the shooting tab and the bracer. The shooting tab comprises a flat, smooth leather protector for the fingers of the shooting hand, which enables the release of the string to be made as smoothly as possible. There is a wide variety of designs available and the choice is a personal one. As an alternative a shooting glove can be used, which normally con-

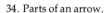

34. Parts of an arrow.
   1. Pile
   2. Cresting
   3. Fletchings
   4. Nock

65

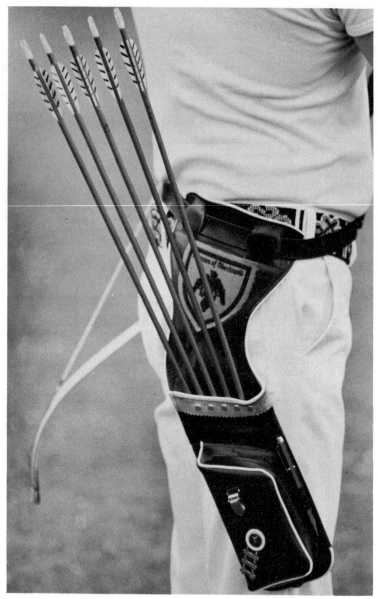

35.   Arrows temporarily stored in a quiver ready for immediate use.

36.   This archer prefers using a shooting glove rather than a tab.

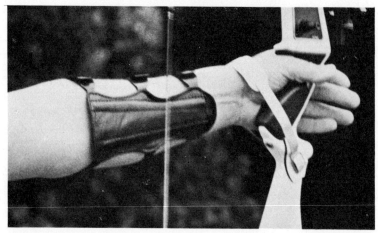

37. The bracer in position, note the string vibrating immediately after release.

38. Behind the waiting line at the Grand National Archery Meeting.

sists of leather finger stalls attached to a skeleton glove fastened at the wrist. Whichever article is used and whatever pattern is chosen, the function is the same. The tab or glove is a very personal accessory and it must fit properly to be effective. A badly fitting tab can have a disastrous effect on the loose, or the release of the arrow, and any discomfort caused by the prolonged use of a tight or ill-fitting glove, is, to say the least, very disconcerting.

Until the proper method of holding a bow is learnt and the correct arm position assumed, the released bow string can often strike the inside of the novice's forearm, and this can and does occasionally happen even with more experienced archers, with painful results. Alternatively the bow string can foul loose clothing and ruin a shot. To prevent either happening a bracer is worn on the bow arm as protection. The basic design of a bracer is a piece of stout leather or stiffened plastic fastened to the arm with a couple of straps. As in the case of shooting tabs there is a wide variety of patterns of bracers to choose from and there is no technical requirement, it is up to the archer to choose a style to suit himself.

We have described in some detail the basic and essential personal equipment required for archery; there are, in addition, a number of other items which archers habitually use, some functional, some useful and others purely decorative. As we progress through the chapters that follow we will refer to many of these items; their acquisition is a matter of taste, desirability or fashion. Sometimes the psychological value of having a special gadget or gimmick is enough to improve shooting, on the principle that if you feel good by the mere possession of such an item then your mental attitude is conditioned and the way is clear for absolute concentration on shooting.

PART TWO

Essential Preliminaries

5

TRAINING

There is a widely held conception that one needs to be an athletic type to draw back a bow, and strangers to archery often doubt that they could become proficient at shooting for reasons of lack of muscle, or those who have followed more gentle pursuits consider themselves not to be up to the energetic requirements of the archery field. We have already hinted more than once that this is far from the case, and let us firmly dispel the notion that one has to be a super-person, physically that is, to achieve success at archery.

Nevertheless there is no harm, and every advantage, in being fit and in so far as archery is concerned one of the finest aids to good shooting is having the feeling of well-being which follows naturally from that condition. Everyone has had the experience of feeling specially good on some days, average on others, and from time to time downright dull. There are certain times, of course, through illness or because of some other specific cause, we feel positively below par, but on such occasions we would not normally be shooting and they can be discounted. Most people do not bother to analyze the extent to which their personal graph of well-being is up or down, or the reason why it is so, but these variations have a critical effect on attitudes, actions, the application of skills and general conduct throughout the day. Human society has always had a way of synthesizing matters of a complex nature into simple terms, particularly those things which cannot be easily comprehended, and the variables to

39. The controlled dynamism of archery is a highly specific form of weight training.

which we have referred are generally dismissed as the moods of a person.

All the emotions, actions and human conditions are related in some way to this complicated and very individual pattern of human experience. What produces the variations in the feeling of personal well-being? There are clearly two main areas of causation, physical and psychological. You may agree that it is simple enough to define the cause of bad temper as stomach ache, or elation as the result of winning the pools, but on the other hand it is not quite so easy to agree a cause, or for that matter even to define one, which is responsible for a constant level of well-being for a whole day's archery. This is the ideal situation, because consistency is the essential quality which leads to good shooting. It is therefore most desirable to probe into the possibility of attaining this agreeable state of mind. It is also relevant to consider what an individual expects, or hopes for, when he or she takes up archery. Some seek little but the pleasure of shooting and the relaxation it offers, and are content to make moderate scores and to progress to a reasonable standard.

Others, after a period of initiation, decide to concentrate on competitive shooting, and their approach is a more deliberate and scientific one. Whatever the aim the general principles of theory and technique apply, and accordingly the guidelines we offer are of a general nature and are applicable to anyone who handles a bow.

How can one achieve the ideal physical condition which helps to create the desired state of mind for archery? If everything is working smoothly physically, then the mind is free of aggravation, it is then that deliberate attempts to concentrate on the task in hand, in this case shooting with a bow and arrow, become easier. Conversely, all of us know only too well the problems of trying to concentrate if our thoughts are diverted to deal with aches, pains or tiredness, let alone interruptions from outside distractions. It is clear then, that to begin with we should attempt to keep our bodies in reasonably good order.

It is good sense to carefully consider a programme which will tone up your general condition and, what is more important, will keep it to a reasonable standard of fitness. We hasten to add that this is an area which has pitfalls for the unwary and over-enthusiastic, and it is emphasized that more harm than good can result unless any unaccustomed exercise is approached with caution and sensibility. In any case it is unnecessary to embark on a crash course of physical training which would be time-wasting and unhelpful to archery. In many ways the actual practice of archery is perfect exercise in itself, and it is therefore logical to first examine the muscular and respiratory activity which occurs during shooting. Then, if these particular matters are understood and any improvement can be effected by planned effort outside archery practice, it follows that shooting itself will be materially assisted.

Many people who have sedentary occupations have a tendency to allow their shoulders to droop, this has the effect of lengthening the muscles in the back, and shortening them in the chest. Holding this position for long can cause physical discomfort, inhibits breathing, and adds to the tiredness often experienced at the end of a working day. Because of the particular activity required when drawing a bow, the back muscles pull the shoulder blades back towards the spinal column, thus those muscles which tend to be lengthened by bad posture over a desk, are encouraged to become shorter by overcoming the resistance to the bow weight, and the chest is expanded which contributes to better breathing. In effect the archer is doing a highly specific form of weight training (see fig. 39). In addition, the action of drawing a bow requires the operation of the shoulder and arm muscles and it is these, and often more particularly the back muscles, that noticeably ache after the first few practical sessions by a beginner. Also the more experienced archer will sometimes feel the effect of re-commencing shooting in the spring after a winter's inactivity. This is why it is a good habit to shoot throughout the winter months if you can, or alternatively, carry out some simple exercises for the back, chest and shoulders, particularly during the off-season.

We have deliberately omitted mention of the muscular control required to perform a number of specific operations during the actual shooting process, for reasons that such matters are better left in their rightful place in the chapters which deal with shooting techniques, and because it is not critical that these mechanisms should be subjected to individual treatment by a programme of physical exercise. On the other hand if the individual feels the necessity of strengthening the joints and extremities that are brought into use, then there is no harm in such an application being employed.

Having some idea of the physical effort expected, let us now examine a bodily function which is too often neglected, that of breathing. Respiration is, generally speaking, the interchange of gases within and without the living organism, oxygen being absorbed into the body and some of the products of combustion, in the form of carbon-dioxide, being removed. By this process the circulating blood is continually being recharged with oxygen. The movement of breathing is initiated by involuntary stimuli which causes the diaphram to contract and other muscles to raise the ribs. Thus if we run for a bus, for example, we automatically breathe more deeply and more quickly, because the respiratory centre, in the brain, has been informed about the extra carbon-dioxide in our blood, which has been produced by the exercising leg muscles, and which has to be dispelled and recharged with oxygen more quickly than normal. Every physical and mental activity uses energy, some, as we have seen, more than others, and the importance of breathing correctly is particularly impor-tant in connection with all forms of sport and other activities which require precise control of bodily movement combined with mental exercise. Archery falls into this category of activity, calling upon a special combination of physical skills and mental discipline.

Everyone, whether merely relaxing, enjoying an energetic pursuit, or carrying out some necessary labour, should learn to breathe properly, and in simple terms this is taking in the right quantity of clean air and expelling enough stale air in a regular fashion at the correct pace. Whereas involuntary respiration will take care of most eventualities, good breathing is dependant on some co-operation from the individual – such as the sometimes forgotten necessity of providing the facility of having fresh air to breathe. Think of the number of hours in a day that you may have denied your body the oxygen it requires by being in smoke-filled, centrally heated, so-called air-conditioned working and living enclosures. Then there is a practical requirement, allowing your breathing mechanism the opportunity of unrestricted working. A moment's thought here will recall the reason why tightly laced Victorian ladies frequently fainted, a practice which is almost as bad as the restriction imposed on the lung cage by bad posture. Possibly the most positive contribution which can be made by the individual, is a conscious and continuous effort to practise good breathing. There are a number of recommended breathing exercises which can be followed and it is up to the individual to seek out the method which is most suitable for him. What should be emphasized, however, is that any exercises undertaken must be controlled, that is to say there is no need, in fact potential harm, in overdoing things for the want of a little professional guidance. It is our intention to point out the way, not to dictate the terms, of these improvement programmes.

40. Superlative archery, like any well performed task, is a pleasure to watch.

Training

Archery is a sport which, if it is done well, looks well, and a study of the way in which those who excel in shooting stand and hold themselves is worth the effort. We shall discuss details of the stance and the composure of the body in the chapters dealing with shooting methods, but for now let us concern ourselves with the general question of posture combined with flexibility of the body, matters which are necessary for the correct practice of archery. The ideal requirements are an erect, evenly balanced posture, combined with flexibility, particularly of the head and neck, shoulders, lumbar region, wrists and fingers. Of course if you know that you are in tip-top condition in these particulars, then do not bother to read on; if, on the other hand, you have the merest doubt that you may be failing even slightly in any one of these aspects, then, providing you want to achieve proficiency with the least physical effort, you should embark on a programme of exercises.

The sought-after posture required for archery is a very natural one, and it is only by a conscious effort to assume it, and to maintain it, can it be automatically achieved. In any case it is not a bad habit to practise good posture, and as a simple expedient one coach has recommended walking as a method for improving posture, with particular emphasis on 'walking tall' whilst doing so. Flexibility of various parts is normally improved by controlled movement exercises rather than muscle building practices, and these movements are well set out in manuals devoted to such matters.

We have identified three principal areas which may need attention if it is decided to embark on a programme preparatory to, and in association with archery practice. They are muscle strengthening, improving breathing, and encouraging the right posture and flexibility, and we have recommended that physical exercise applied in different ways can materially assist in overcoming shortcomings in such matters. It is also worth while considering isometric exercises as suitable alternatives to the otherwise rather more strenuous physical activity that may be adopted. These exercises pit one muscle or part of the body against another, or against an immovable object, in a strong but motionless pressing, pushing, pulling, flexing or contracting action. One advantage of these exercises is that many of them can be carried out perfectly satisfactorily whilst sitting in a car or at a desk, and no excuse can be made for neglecting them because of lack of time or facilities.

Throughout the whole process of applying physical improvement programmes it is absolutely vital that you should first have complete knowledge of yourself. Your shortcomings should be accurately assessed and the remedies should be applied with a precise awareness of just how much is required to effect the desired result. By adopting a modest toning up programme there is, in addition to the benefits of better health and physique, a psychological advantage, and a big step forward will have been taken towards creating the right archery mood. This is a question which has been studied at length by those who are dedicated to training for competition. Several different aspects of the mental approach to archery have been analyzed and published as part of specialist training manuals, and the logical approach for the newcomer is to seek out and read the varying expositions on the subject, carefully noting the particular aims of each.

The starting point for any considerations of the psychological factor is the straightforward premise that the repetition of the act of shooting an arrow properly is primarily dependant on mental discipline. The pattern of this disciplinary process involves decisions concerning every practical stage in the rhythm of shooting, plus a series of abstract matters covering such aspects as judgment of timing and self-analysis of performance. If we add to this an overall pattern of concentration, the rejection of outside influences, and an unemotional reaction to success or failure for each shot, we have some idea of the level of mental discipline which has to be achieved for a top performance. The consistency of this sought-after mental approach is possibly the most difficult of attainments, because of the changes which can occur throughout a day's shooting which alter the personal mood. There is little doubt that if our physical condition is in good order, then a consistency in the pattern of mental discipline becomes more easy to acquire.

41. The inner calm of a world champion is revealed by Darell Pace in this meditative pose at the Montreal Olympics.

It is one thing to theorize on the ideal psychological requirements for a championship performance, it is another matter to
decide how such a level of mental discipline can be approached,
or, more particularly at this stage, how a less advanced archer can
create something of this higher aim for the particular form and
standard of archery he requires. The answer to this is to begin a
personal programme of deliberate thought patterns which can be
repeated over and over again when you are shooting. Be aware of
your own capabilities and limitations, do not expect to achieve an
outstanding improvement overnight, but be content with
gradual advancement. Above all train your mind to think out
archery problems in a deliberate manner. Take one aspect at a
time, and by resolving it mentally the problem is more than half
settled.

A hitherto unexplored area of thought is represented by what
is called bio-rhythmics, where it is maintained that our best peaks
of activity occur in a predictable fashion, and if those high spots
can be sufficiently identified and utilized accordingly, then our
accomplishments are that much improved. The theory has deep
implications in that a multitude of variables can be produced by
influences of a physiological or psychological nature, and that the
rhythmic pattern has as yet only been identified as a series in time
and cannot be induced. However once the problems of timing
can be resolved, and the maximum condition can be assumed by
the individual on command, then its application to archery could
be realized. Until then, regretfully, we shall have to hope that our
bio-rhythmic peaks happen when we need them most on the
shooting line. Despite the clear problems these theories present
us with, it is possible that some archers have, unwittingly, found
the solution, and can induce bio-rhythmic peaks. In such cases
the identity of these fortunates does not remain a secret for long,
their names can be found consistently at the top of international
prize lists.

The final topic to be discussed in this particular chapter is one
which has received very little attention in archery books, that is
outside France, and which we shall designate very generally as
dietary considerations. Let us argue thus: if, on taking up archery

you are going to the expense of buying valuable archery equipment, joining a club, taking the trouble of investigating the many facets of training, including physical exercises, shooting techniques and the mental approach, then surely it is worth while reviewing the all-important question of diet. It is not for us to set down dietary formulas or to propose calorie-based, low carbohydrate or other systems of controlled eating, or for that matter go so far as to give recipes for properly balanced mid-competition snacks, as have actually been published. Instead we will suggest a way of examining your own diet to satisfy yourself that you are supplying your body with adequate and properly balanced fuel to perform all your newly acquired archery skills.

In recent years the general public have become more conscious of the biochemistry of eating and there is a widespread interest in the necessity of understanding diet. So far as archery is concerned it should go without saying that to eat a heavy Sunday lunch accompanied by a bottle of wine and then expect to do well on the archery field in the afternoon is a hope rarely fulfilled, as such preparation would be disastrous both to the score and to the digestion, and yet this is not unknown. Conversely, to feel hungry, or thirsty for that matter, half-way through a competition round is introducing a physiological disturbance and a mental diversion into what otherwise might have been a regular pattern of shooting, thus risking a major disruption of that process and a performance which might have been better.

Contemplate on the fact that man, with all his ingenuity, is the only animal who does not know instinctively how to select his food. This is one reason why the science of dietetics has evolved. It is therefore logical to assume that if we have no knowledge of when to eat, what to eat and why, we are liable to harm ourselves through ignorance. In fact scientific surveys reveal that around fifty per cent of the active adult population are overweight due to incorrect diet. It is true that the majority of studies in this field have been directed towards weight-reducing diets, but nonetheless the knowledge on which they are based consists of scientific evidence as to what proper feeding should be. The dietary requirement of an individual depends on several factors, the physique and health of that person and the physical and mental demands which are made over any period in question. This is a highly specialized subject and one that has been presented in numerous books and articles devoted to nutrition and dietetics, most of which incorporate a sound basic understanding of the physiological principles involved.

These comments are intended to act as a reminder of how important diet can be in assisting the programme of toning up, making it possible to shoot with that extra confidence and enjoyment, which after all, is the whole object of this literary exercise.

6

VISION

We tend to take for granted the faculty of vision, without which, of course, there would be no archery. This is an essential aspect which is often neglected, and a full understanding of the importance of the optical functions and the accompanying problems of aiming, will make all the difference between accurate shooting and inconsistency.

There are a number of defects in acuity from which a fairly large proportion of us suffer, such as hypermetropia (far-sightedness) myopia (near-sightedness), asthenopia (eye-fatigue), astigmatism and so on. These are the more common refracting errors and are usually correctible with suitable spectacles, the only necessity being that they should be of the correct curved type. They must have the same power at the edge of the lens as they do at the centre, as a sight is often taken off-centre through the lens. However if eye defects are not cared for they can undermine the archer's enthusiasm, and a periodic check will result in benefit, not only to the performance with a bow and arrow, but also to the general well-being of the individual.

There is absolutely no reason why a person who normally wears correctly prescribed spectacles, or for that matter contact lenses, should be at any disadvantage on the archery field. We have emphasized 'correctly prescribed' spectacles as the current rules of shooting prohibit the wearing of microhole glasses while shooting, as this would constitute an additional form of sighting device. [Rule 103 (b)]. So many physiological and psychological

85

aspects are closely linked and it has long been recognized that if the mind is clear of worry or tension, higher standards of archery are more accessible, and what is more the enjoyment is greater. Bad vision can be a worry, which can manifest itself in nervous tension, resulting in a poor performance, disappointing to the beginner, unsatisfactory to his instructor and a constant source of frustration to those who persevere and never progress. The importance of your eyes working properly for you cannot be over-emphasized, and they must not be neglected.

The optical mechanism allows for automatic clarity of vision for subjects under scrutiny at close quarters, middle or long distances, and this is a facility which is in constant use in archery. If both eyes are used a situation occurs which is a phenomenon of binocular vision, and which has a particular application for the archer. There are two retinal images of every external object, and since these images are projected outwards into space as external images, there must be two external images of every object. In fact

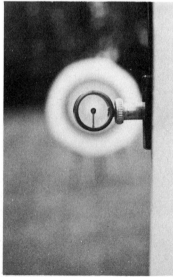 

42. A ring bow-sight with central post and bead, held on the centre of the target.

43. When we require it the target is brought into clear focus.

all objects are seen double, except under special conditions, but the object is seen single when the two images of it are superimposed and coincide at the same spot in space. This is known as the law of corresponding points, and the importance of this becomes apparent when the problems of accurately sighting with a bow and arrow on a target as much as 100 yards distant or even further are examined.

The point of sight, in our case the distant target, is brought into clear focus when we require it, and it is then seen as a single object. But objects above and below it or to one side or the other of the point of sight, may possibly be seen single also, and the sum of these points which are seen single, while the point of sight remains unchanged, is called the horopter. There is, therefore, an obvious benefit in looking at distant objects with both eyes open, and the advantage, in so far as archery practice is concerned, should be apparent. However, when a sight is taken with an arrow at full draw both eyes can be open or the disengaged eye closed: in either case only one eye is fully used, the one known as the dominant or controlling eye, and if the other is used as well it lags behind the first in strength and optical correctness.

On taking up archery the first practical matter to be attended to is to check which is your controlling eye. In the majority of people this is normally the right, in some it is the left and in a very small minority neither, but this is very rare. There is one simple method of ascertaining which is your controlling eye: hold both hands out in front of you at arms' length, and form a peephole with the thumbs and fingers an inch or so across and look at a distant object through the opening. Now, without moving your head, close one eye and then the other. Whichever eye still sees the distant object through the opening is your controlling eye. This eye, doing your sighting for you, is naturally of the utmost importance. A right-handed person (the bow held in the left hand) whose *left* eye is dominant, is going to have some difficulty in shooting, for the reason that because of the visual phenomenon which takes place (physiological diplopia) it is impossible to accurately line up sight, arrow and target, and any aiming corrections made will be offset by this optical falsity. If, of course,

44. Checking the dominant eye, right eye open (the controlling eye).

45. Checking the dominant eye, left eye open (right eye is the controlling eye).

the archer is left-handed (the bow held in the right hand) there would be no problem, and for those who have difficulty in this respect the handling of the bow must be reversed in the very early stages of shooting. Provided the archer is aware of which eye is the controlling one, and shoots left or right-handed accordingly, it will also be found advantageous to practise shooting with both eyes open, for in addition to the reasons already given, this will enable the dominant eye to take over. It is possible to overcome eye dominancy by training the inferior eye to work, but this would depend on constant and concentrated practice of a specialized nature. Throughout this book we shall assume that our remarks are addressed to right-handed archers, that is to say those who normally shoot with the bow held in the left hand, with the right eye dominant.

There are a number of other interesting aspects concerned with vision which relate to various forms of archery. For example the extent to which you can see up or down and to the side while looking straight ahead, is your visual field and utilizes peripheral vision. This field is used when leading or aiming off at moving targets and it warns of approach from either side. In Field Archery the ability to judge distances is invaluable and the intricacies of depth perception are worthy of additional study. It is possible to go fishing with a bow and arrows and in this case optical illusions, due to the properties of refraction in water, have to be overcome.

What concerns us more particularly however, are the problems of aiming with a bow and arrow. This is a subject which is often dealt with only briefly, and consequently many beginners are unable to fully understand the principles involved, with a result that they experience disappointment in their early efforts to hit a target without sufficient knowledge to control their shots or to correct what might have been a simple error.

It is all very well for a beginner, in the early stages of archery with a hundred and one things to think about, to be told that it matters little whether he hits the target or not; this may be so, in fact emphasis on the correct method of shooting is of primary importance to begin with, but there is no doubt of the psychological encouragement in hitting the target, even at short range. Therefore it is quite important that early lessons in theory should be devoted to aiming.

It is assumed that the arrows used are the correct length, weight and spine for the bow, and that any discrepancies resulting from faults in technique are discounted. Generally speaking, except for very short distances, an arrow does not travel in a straight line. As it loses speed it starts to fall in a low curve and this part of its flight is called its Trajectory. The Trajectory can vary according to the elevation at which the arrow was discharged, by its velocity, and by wind currents. If this is viewed from above the path taken by the arrow is the Line of Flight, and this also can be deflected from a straight line by wind variations. We have already discussed the erratic initial course of the arrow produced by the phenomenon known as the Archer's Paradox. If all the variables which affect the flight of an arrow are added together one can begin to appreciate the skill required to control and direct each successive shot accurately to the target. The equipment manufacturers have done their ballistic sums and have produced bows and arrows which will react to the best advantage to all these variables. From that point it is up to the archer to study and develop the means of properly controlling his shooting to achieve the maximum result.

The course of the arrow has to be initially calculated so that it reaches home on the target. This initial calculation is the result of trial and error, and it is based on the fact that there are several constant factors by means of which the pattern of aiming is constructed. There are, in fact, several methods of aiming for different forms of shooting all based on the same basic principles. The first method, which is by far the most predominant, is that

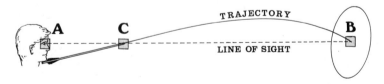

46.   The theory of aiming for Target Archery.

normally used for all target shooting. The constant factors which comprise the basis of aiming are, the eye of the archer (A), the target or aiming mark (B), and the sighting mark (C). These combined with the Angle of Elevation and Line of Direction of the arrow, which is pivoted from a constant location, provide a reasonably accurate method of aiming a bow.

For precise repetition of shooting an arrow after a correct aim has been taken, several other matters have to be performed. These matters, such as drawing the arrow back to exactly the same distance each time, nocking the arrow on to the string at the same spot, and the all-important operation of the loose, will be discussed in detail in later chapters. For the present we will examine the ideal aiming arrangement assuming that all these matters have been properly taken care of.

When the Line of Sight cuts the Trajectory of the arrow exactly at the point (pile) of the arrow at full draw, it means that the pile

47. The view of the target with the point of the arrow used as an aiming mark.

48. The view when a sight is taken with a sighting device.

of the arrow can then be placed visually on the 'gold' (the central ring of the target), which will be hit by the released arrow. This is the ideal aiming situation and there is clearly a series of 'exact' positions of bow, arrow and target when this is bound to occur, which depend on the difference in size and strength of the equipment and the distance at which the target is set up. However such an arrangement will rarely obtain as the archer is restricted to shooting at pre-arranged distances. Let us assume that the arrow overshoots the target; some adjustment has then to be made and the only aspect that can change is the elevation of the arrow. In this case it has to be depressed to enable a lesser distance to be reached. With all the other positions remaining constant this will result in the view of the target appearing 'higher' in relationship to the arrow. If a mark is made on the bow limb it will be seen that this aiming position can be assumed time after time, and if an adjustable sighting device is fitted at this point on the bow an even more accurate control can be attained. To help the archer correct his sight at the beginning of a round he is allowed six non-scoring sighters, which we have already referred to.

Most modern bows are provided with sights which perform the same function as a foresight on a rifle, but unlike that weapon a bow has no backsight. The variety of sights now available on the market range from a simple sliding pin to precision-made items capable of micro-adjustment. A recent improvement has been introduced which involves extending the sight assembly on a bar to a point six inches or more in front of the bow. This has the effect of diminishing the problems associated with the law of corresponding points, in that the focal point relationship between sight and target draw closer together. The sliding sight is calibrated for easy adjustment and positions for various distances can be quickly established, but they will vary slightly according to weather conditions. A following wind, blowing down the range towards the targets, will lift the arrow and extend its range, so that the sight used will be a little higher than normal. Alternatively a head wind, from the targets, will depress and shorten the flight of the arrow, necessitating the use of a lower sighting mark.

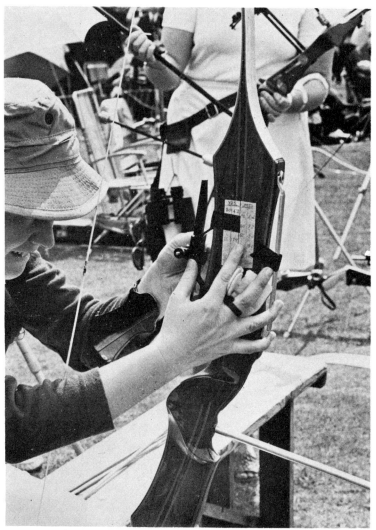

49. A scale of sight positions in yards and metres on the side of this bow helps the archer to select the correct adjustment for his bowsight.

Cross winds may affect the line, and to correct this lateral adjustments can be made to the sight pin position.

50. The bowsight assembly on this bow is attached to the extremity of an extension bar which projects in front of the bow.

The method we have described is that normally used for Target Archery and modifications of these arrangements are used in other forms of shooting. For example in Clout Shooting, where the distances are much greater than in Target Archery, a mark on the lower limb of the bow is often used, this is known as shooting 'underhand'. Alternatively, for this particular form of shooting, a small button, called a 'kisser', is attached to the string, and if this is properly located and brought back to touch the mouth the result will be that the arrow is drawn back to a lower position than normally. The effect of this will be to elevate the angle of the arrow and a greater distance will be achieved.

Another method of aiming, which utilizes the principles that we have described, is useful for developing a good shooting form, and as such is an excellent method for a beginner. This is where a fixed 'point of aim' is employed, which can be a marker having a diameter of no more than 7·5-cm, and which must not protrude more than 15-cm above the ground. [Rule 103 (d)]. It is

51. Shooting underhand by means of a mark on the lower limb of the bow which acts as a sight.

52. The use of a kisser to establish a constant location for the string, popularly used in most forms of archery.

placed on the ground in line with the target, at a position which, when it is used as a sighting mark, will enable arrows to hit the

53. Point of aim shooting, sometimes known as the space picture method of aiming, where the mark 'B' is an imaginary spot away from the target. The anchor point 'A' is high; normally used for Field Archery.

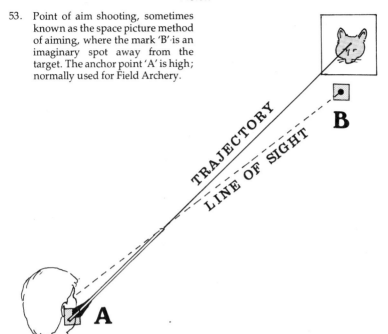

centre of the target. In this case the pile of the arrow is used for aiming and a mechanical sighting device on the bow is not used. Adjustments are effected by moving the point of aim, the other factors remaining constant as before.

The adjustments which we have described, which include alterations to the sight pin, varying the angle of the arrow, changing the position of the point of aim, etc, are the compensating factors which have to be made because the eye cannot be lined up directly with the flight of the arrow. The instinctive method of aiming ideally requires the arrow to be brought more in line with the eye, and to achieve this it is drawn back to a higher position or 'Anchor Point' than in the recognized Target Archery method. This form of shooting is used extensively in Field Shooting and in hunting, and although there is a considerable amount of literature dealing with this subject the only satisfactory way of understanding it is to experiment with it. Instinctive shooting is really no more than what it says it is, where the direction, angle, power and aim of the shot are all co-ordinated in an instinctive fashion. The basic principles of aiming which we described earlier must be divorced from the instinctive method, and if an archer is willing to spend a lot of time developing and maintaining proficiency in this style it can be a very satisfactory accomplishment. It is also a method of aiming utilized for shooting near vertically at the Popinjay mast to hit a target ninety feet in the air.

There are no rules which can be laid down, or for that matter suggested, which will provide a reasonable basis for instinctive shooting, in the way that the precepts of aiming can be determined for other forms of archery. In many ways comparisons can be drawn between being a good instinctive shot and being an accurate thrower of stones, it is a matter of using natural instincts and regarding the low velocity missile as a projection of the human body and brain. In a later chapter we describe another method of shooting which is more often than not employed for Field Archery, but for the present we have explained sufficiently those matters concerning aiming to enable the beginner to proceed with the business of learning to shoot.

There are a number of other practical matters which have to be perfected before the aiming methods which we have described can be brought into practice. The theory of aiming is a subject worth studying with some care, for by an intelligent application of its principles and by carefully putting them to practical use, a more consistent pattern of shooting will result.

7

PREPARATION

In this chapter we gather together a series of practical matters other than actual shooting, which can be considered as a checklist of essentials and desirables, including such matters as field and target regulations, the handling of equipment, and some of the paraphenalia that archers use. We have already mentioned the fact that there are several different forms of shooting, the most popular undoubtedly being Target Archery, and the bulk of this book is concerned with that activity. In chapter three we mentioned 'rounds' which form the basis of target shooting, and those rounds which are officially recognized by G.N.A.S., and which are used in competitive shooting by clubs and societies affiliated to that body, are listed overleaf. [Rules 106(a), 300, and 510(a)].

The target for shooting these rounds consists of a boss about 4 inches (10·16-cm) thick and approximately 4 feet (122 cm) in diameter, made of tightly coiled straw rope. On this is stretched a target face of canvas or similar material painted with scoring rings. [Rule 100]. The arrangement is as follows: a circle in the centre measuring 9³/₅ inches (24·4 cm) is ringed by four concentric bands each 4⁴/₅ inches (12·2 cm) wide. From the centre outwards the colours are yellow (called the 'gold'), red, blue, black and white, their scoring values being 9, 7, 5, 3 and 1 respectively. This is usually referred to as the British standard 5-zone face. Two sizes of target face are used for shooting under international rules, each at different shooting distances. A 122 cm target face is

TARGET ROUNDS

Name of Round	Number of arrows						
	100 yds	80 yds	60 yds	50 yds	40 yds	30 yds	20 yds
York	72	48	24				
St George	36	36	36				
New Western	48	48					
New National	48	24					
Hereford (Bristol I)		72	48	24			
Long Western		48	48				
Long National		48	24				
Albion		36	36	36			
Windsor			36	36	36		
American			30	30	30		
Western			48	48			
National			48	24			

JUNIOR ROUNDS

Bristol I			72	48	24		
Bristol II				72	48	24	
Bristol III					72	48	24
Bristol IV						72	48	24
Short Windsor				36	36	36	
St Nicholas					48	36	

METRIC ROUNDS

	90m	70m	60m	50m	40m	30m	20m	10m
FITA (Gentlemen)	36	36		36		36		
FITA (Ladies) (Metric I)		36	36	36		36		
Long Metric (Gentlemen)	36	36						
Long Metric (Ladies)		36	36					
Short Metric				36		36		

JUNIOR ROUNDS

	90m	70m	60m	50m	40m	30m	20m	10m
Metric I		36	36	36		36		
Metric II			36	36	36	36		
Metric III				36	36	36	36	
Metric IV					36	36	36	36

INDOOR ROUNDS

	20yds	30m	25m	18m
Portsmouth (60cm target face)		60		
Worcester (40cm target face)		60		
Stafford (80cm target face)			72	
FITA Round I (40cm target face)				30
FITA Round II (60cm target face)			30	

Notes

(a) In every round the longer or longest distance is shot first, and the shorter or shortest distance last.

(b) When FITA and Metric rounds are shot, FITA Rules apply.

(c) A FITA round may be shot in one day or over two consecutive days.

(d) All other rounds to be shot in one day (except in the case of a championship of more than one day's duration).

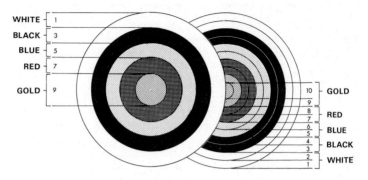

54. The standard 122 cm 5-zone target and the international 10-zone target face.

used for distances of 90, 70 and 60 metres, and an 80 cm face is used for distances of 50 and 30 metres. Both these faces are divided into 10 zones, each colour of the standard 5-zone face being halved, the scoring values then ranging from 10 for the inner gold to 1 for the outermost ring of the white.

The target is erected on a wooden stand of a height such that its exact centre (known as the pin-hole), is 51¼ inches (130 cm) vertically above the ground, inclined at an angle of 15 degrees, [Rule 101 (a)] and it should be securely anchored to prevent it from being blown over. [Rule 101 (c)]. The ideal archery range consists of a level area of closely cropped grass in a reasonably sheltered position. In the most favoured arrangement, in the northern hemisphere, the ground is laid out on a north-and-south axis, and the targets are set up at the northern end. There should be a safety zone of at least 25 yards to the rear and 10 yards to the side of the targets. [Rule 100 (i)].

Archers stand astride a clearly defined shooting line, or mark, to shoot, which is measured back from a point vertically below the pin-hole of the target. [Rule 101 (e)]. There is a waiting line at least 5 yards behind the shooting line, [Rule 101 (h)] and the space between these lines must be kept clear except for archers walking to and from the shooting line. The field arrangements, which are those laid down for tournaments, are the basis of what can be expected at club shoots, and to avoid the lengthy task of

55. These targets are securely anchored by means of cords, to safeguard arrows in the event of high winds blowing targets from stands.

56. An added luxury on a well-kept archery ground are mowing lanes which
assist the archers to select their targets.

measuring out the ground each time shooting takes place,
various time and labour saving ideas are put into use. For
example, permanent distance markers can sometimes be sunk
into the ground below grass cutting level, or perhaps a
non-stretchable cord, having the various distances clearly
marked on it, is quickly run out to locate the positions of targets
and shooting line.

The order in which archers shoot at their respective targets is
shown on a Target List, normally No. 3 on a target automatically
becomes Target Captain and No. 4 the Lieutenant. The Captain is
responsible for the orderly conduct of shooting on his particular
target, and it is he who is also responsible for seeing that the
scores are correctly recorded, which are counter-checked by the

57. Arrows must be marked with the archers names or initials to assist identification when scores are taken.

Lieutenant. [Rules 103 (b)(i) and 105 (b)]. Each arrow, which must be marked with the archer's name or initials, [Rule 103 (a)] is identified by its owner and its value called in sequence in the manner which we have already described. [Rule 106 (b)]. There are specific rules covering any doubtful or unusual situations which may arise concerning scoring. For example, what does an arrow score if it hits and remains embedded in another, or what is the score if an arrow touches two colours on the target? Perhaps an arrow bounces off the target or even passes through it. These and other special circumstances are allowed for in the various sections of Rule 106. A full understanding of the method of scoring, which is extremely simple, and of the action required when unexpected circumstances arise, is an essential part of the beginner's training.

In chapter four we described the essential equipment for an archer, and before we give some hints as to how that equipment, or more familiarly 'tackle', should be cared for, let us complete the catalogue of what the average archer may accummulate as

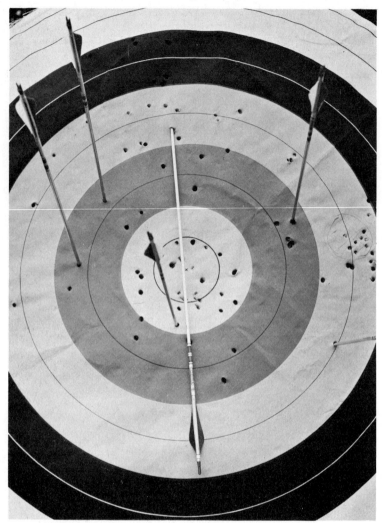

58.   A 'hanger' which could be a danger to other shots.

items which he could not do without. One such item, which is traditionally part of an archer's outfit, is the tassel. This accessory, slung from the archer's belt, has a utilitarian as well as

59. The Judge stops the shooting and replaces the hanger properly in the target.

60. The tassel, more ornamental than useful, usually made in club colours.

a decorative function, and often attracts comment from the uninitiated. For centuries it has been used to clean arrows of any wet or dirt which would otherwise affect their flight, and nowadays tassels are made up in club colours, a central register of which is maintained for clubs in this country.

Today most archers use a quiver. For Target Archery several types are in general use, normally slung from the belt at a convenient angle so that arrows temporarily stored there are readily accessible. It can be a simple tube or an elaborate work of leather-craft according to the fancy of the individual. For Field Shooting and hunting a quiver designed to be slung on the archer's back is more popular. The disadvantage of the hanging

61. An example of the wide variety of quivers which can be seen at any archery meeting. Note also the personal score pad hanging from the belt.

type quiver in Field Shooting is that it is liable to become entangled in bushes and undergrowth, whereas the back quiver is nicely tucked away close to the body and cannot swing about. Another form of quiver is known as a ground quiver. This is designed to be stuck into the ground to provide a convenient means of resting the bow and storing the arrows whilst the archer waits his turn to shoot. This simple gadget plays an important part, not only in keeping the shooting ground tidy, but also in preventing damage to bows and arrows otherwise left carelessly lying around.

There is no objection to the use of binoculars, or monoculars, to identify individual shots, which is found to be very helpful by many archers, enabling critical corrections to be made arrow by arrow. They can be used other than when the archer is shooting, otherwise their use could be a transgression of Rule 103 (c) which forbids the use of lenses or prisms in bowsights. Archers are

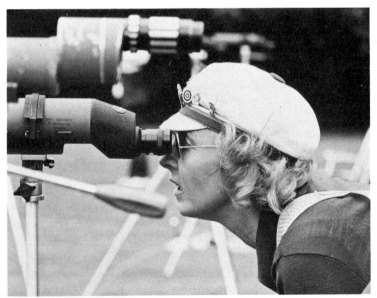

62. The use of elaborate monoculars, telescopes or binoculars has become commonplace, enabling archers to precisely locate each arrow on the target.

particularly apt to devise and use gadgets both ingenious and frivolous, and any shooting line can provide a crop of such extra items which do not appear in any text book or equipment catalogue. They are not essentials, but so long as they provide the means of better enjoyment of the sport and do not contravene the rules of shooting in force at the time, there is no objection to them.

Regular maintenance of an archer's equipment ensures that it is always in good condition and safe to use. A loose feather or a frayed string may sound trifles, but such things can be the cause of erratic shooting as well as a bad temper. Before and after every shooting session it is a good habit to check your tackle. See that all fletchings are secure, make sure that no arrows are bent, check the string for fraying, and ensure that the serving and nocking points are intact.

63.   It is important to protect arrows from bending by carefully drawing them from targets and this is a practical method of doing this.

64. Arrows can also be bent if they are carelessly dragged from the ground, it is better to carefully withdraw them straight back in line.

The serving on a string is an additional whipping with thread around the loops at each end and for six or eight inches or so at the centre of the string, to prevent fraying by friction at the loops and from wear at the point where fingers are hooked over the string. The nocking point is an extra wrapping of finer thread, at one time waxed silk was used, but now it is usually dental floss, and this provides an exact location for the arrow each time it is nocked on to the string. The thickness of the nocking point is critical, as it has to accommodate the arrow notch (or 'nock') just firmly enough for the arrow to hang from the string but free enough for it to leave the string on release without any resistance.

When not in use store your tackle neatly and safely. Minor do-it-yourself repairs, which are invariably carried out as a routine or in an emergency, can easily be picked up by seeking the advice of other more experienced archers. It is a matter of

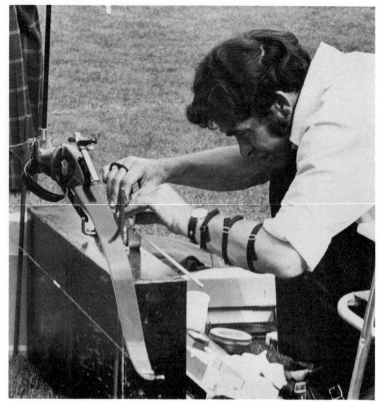

65. On the spot repairs: replacing a damaged fletching between ends.

common sense and practicability rather than specially acquired skills which enable the most inexperienced archer to cope admirably in looking after his own tackle. It is almost instinctive for an archer to be practical and this quality is an undoubted asset. Apart from the actual making of bows and arrows, the general maintenance and the handling of these simple but fascinating weapons can easily be managed, however it is no job for the careless or hamfisted. First know your tackle – then care for it; such devotion will be repaid with faithful service, and many pleasurable hours of healthful recreation will be experienced, combined with a special, quite personal, exhilaration

112

when man, bow and arrow work as one.

Once the correct equipment has been chosen with a little forethought and guidance, a routine of shooting based on sound principles can begin. As a matter of preparation, the first practical operation that has to be performed is bracing the bow, or stringing it ready for action, and as with everything else concerned with archery, this must be done properly and in a prescribed fashion. There are three common methods practised today by which a bow is braced, the choice of which depends largely on the type of bow being used.

The first method is most suitable for bows without recurved limbs, such as self-wood or solid fibre-glass bows, and it is the typical method used with longbows. Stand with the feet about a foot and a half apart and take the bow in the right hand about the grip. Place the end of the lower limb against the instep of the right foot, not on the ground, and cant the bow across the body with the belly, or concave side of the bow, to the left. One loop of the string should be in place on the lower nock and the other should be slipped over the top end of the bow and should rest loosely about four to five inches from the bow tip. Place the left hand, palm down, on the bow towards its upper end, and take the loose loop between the fingers so that it can be easily slipped up the bow limb towards the nock. Now simultaneously pull with the right hand and push with the left; this will bend the bow evenly and the upper string loop can be eased into position in its nock. Gently relax the tension and examine the braced bow to ensure that the string lies centrally along the axis of the bow and check the bracing height. The bow is now ready for shooting.

The second method is used extensively with recurved composite bows which would be difficult to manage by the first method. The string is placed in position on the lower nock, and with the feet some eighteen inches apart, the hollow portion of the lower recurved bow limb is placed in front of the left ankle. The belly of the bow is now positioned behind the right leg and the handle riser is located against the back of the thigh. With the string held taut in the left hand, and making sure that it is correctly in position on the lower nock, the upper end of the bow is now

113

drawn forward against the back of the right thigh with the right hand. The upper loop of the string can now be slipped on to its nock, the tension gradually relaxed, and the bow examined for

66. Bracing a simple bow.

67. Bracing a composite bow.

position of string and bracing height as before. This method must be used very carefully to avoid twisting the bow limbs during the flexing movement.

A safe and popular alternative method of bracing a composite bow is by the use of a 'bow stringer'. Several types have appeared on the market but one of the simplest and easiest to operate consists of an extra long string provided with a pouch at one end and a large reinforced loop at the other. To use it, the pouch, which encloses a small loop, is placed in position over the bow nock of the upper limb and the larger loop is slipped over the lower limb. The string is then slack and long enough for one foot to be placed over it with the bow held horizontal, string down. Next hold the upper loop in place, and as you straighten up, which will have the effect of bending the bow, slip the bow string proper into place, gently relax tension and check the position of

68.   Bracing a composite bow by means of a 'bow-stringer'.

69. Checking that the bowstring is securely in position and that it is properly located in line with the centre of the bow.

the string as in the other methods described. The advantage of using a bow-stringer is that it prevents twisting of the bow limbs.

When a bow is braced the taut string holds the bow limbs slightly in tension. If a view is taken along the line of the string it will be seen to exactly bisect the whole length of the bow – if it does not, then something is seriously wrong. Possibly one of the loops is badly located over the bow tip, or, more seriously, the bow limbs are twisted. In the latter case there is nothing to be done but to return the bow to the supplier. Let us hope that everything is ship-shape. Now observe the distance between the bow at its centre and the string, this is an important measurement which is taken at right-angles from the string to the belly of the bow or to an indicator specially provided by the maker. This is known as the bracing height which must conform to the specification suggested by the manufacturer, and it should remain constant at all times. Most bow strings are made to an accurate standard to fit specific bows and rarely require any more adjustment than a twist or two one way or another to shorten or

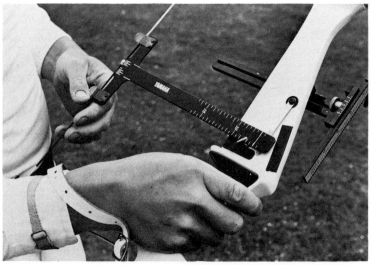

70.   A useful gauge to check the accuracy of the bracing height of the string.

Preparation

lengthen them slightly, so that the bracing height can be regulated by raising or lowering.

Having successfully braced a bow, adjusted the bracer, fitted a finger tab or shooting glove, and buckled on a belt and quiver, everything is now in order to begin shooting. All is now ready for the next and most important stage, that of discovering the art of archery by practical experience. Already we have dealt with an appreciable amount of detail involving administration and the theory of archery. Most of this material which you have patiently studied so far usually appears in conjunction with a description of shooting methods, but in our case we felt that these first few chapters would provide a useful reference section separate from the more practical aspects of archery. In the next few chapters we shall guide you through each stage of shooting with a bow and arrow, including the recommended Basic Method of learning how to shoot and more detailed notes on shooting techniques, all of which should enable a novice to learn the rudiments and advance to a reasonable standard. For those more familiar with the practice of archery there is an opportunity to pick up extra guidance in order that individual performances can be improved.

PART THREE

Techniques of Shooting

8

STANDING

The overall aim when shooting in a bow, particularly in Target Archery, is to achieve absolute consistency of position, movement and timing for every individual shot. It is only through a conscious effort to achieve this consistency that the basis of good shooting is established. With practice many of the necessary preliminary aspects can be performed automatically, but even the best archers find that from time to time they have to critically review their shooting style. A bad habit is hard to break, it is easier to get it right to begin with until it becomes second nature.

There is no formal method of shooting which must be followed. It may well be that some archers have succeeded in achieving a reasonable proficiency by self-taught methods, or by emulating one of the many schools of shooting. However a great deal of time and effort by trained coaches and instructors has resulted in the emergence of what is known as the Basic Method of shooting. This is to be commended both as a satisfactory system for teaching beginners and as a set of techniques which forms the basis for more advanced archers to improve their performance. Individuals often introduce variations to the Basic Method; there is no harm in that – provided the results pay off in terms of better shooting. Nevertheless when changes, no matter how small, appear to make no difference to your shooting, it is time to go back to basics. In fact it is a good rule, applicable to both novices and the more experienced, to regularly assess your own shooting techniques in accordance with the Basic Method. The

71.   The correct basic standing position.

72. Establishing a proper alignment with the target.

chapters that follow incorporate the Basic Method together with more detailed supplementary notes for progressive archery.

For the practice of Target Archery the archer should stand astride the shooting line and at right-angles to it, in an upright, comfortable and relaxed position with the feet a reasonable distance apart, the recommended distance being about the same width as the shoulders. The weight of the body should be distributed evenly on both feet. Careful adjustment of this

125

position is essential until the shoulders are aligned in such a way that an imaginary straight line drawn through them is directed at the target or aiming mark.

It is advisable for the novice to check the standing position so that the correct alignment with the target is established. This can be done by standing as already described, looking straight ahead, then raise the arms sideways level with the shoulders and, with the left eye closed (assuming that your right eye is dominant) and turning the head to the left, look at the target. It is important to remember that the head must turn without tilting and that the view is taken with the dominant eye. Arms and shoulders should now be exactly in line with the target, then all is well. If not then move the feet one way or another until the right position has been established.

It is worth while taking care to check this position each time you shoot until you are confident that you are standing correctly. The direction of a line drawn through your feet in relation to the shoulder line is of minimal importance so long as you stand in a relaxed and comfortable position. Having taken a satisfactory stance the position of each foot can be fixed by the use of foot

73.   The use of foot markers which can be left in position during a round.

126

markers, which must not exceed 1 cm in height. [Rule 103 (h)] It is important that the correct shooting position should remain static, that is to say there is no move from it, and the same position should be adopted each time shooting takes place.

Once the correct stance has been taken, the whole process of shooting relies on several distinct and controlled physical movements, and it is advisable to consider these carefully. When the head is turned towards the target, and this is always the case when shooting is in progress, it must remain upright and under no circumstances should it be tilted sideways or backwards. Changing the position of the head also changes the angle of the eyes, and as we have already noted when the theory of aiming was discussed, the eye position is one of the constant factors that enables the consistency necessary for accurate shooting to be attained. The shoulders must be maintained in a horizontal position and in line with the target, and any alteration from this position can have disastrous results in the way a bow is drawn and in the direction of the released arrow.

We have already described the part played by the back muscles, and it is as well to recall that they control all movements which lift and draw the bow, and a conscious effort in the early days to make back muscles work properly will pay dividends later. Once the bow is at full draw, the finer details of which we shall discuss in due course, its final alignment is made by a minimal movement of the upper body from the waist. It will be seen how necessary fitness preparation can be when these various restrained and precisely controlled bodily movements are studied, and it is particularly relevant that these principles are understood from the beginning.

The way that a bow is held is important, and it is now time to make sure that this is done properly. The principle that governs the best position of the hand is the fact that it should act as a pivot, from which the two bow limbs bend equally, and the point of balance, the true centre of the bow, is usually just over an inch below the arrow shelf when the bow is braced. The majority of composite bows incorporate sculptured hand grips which guide the hand into the correct position, but fibre-glass bows, which are highly recommended for less advanced shooting, are provided with little or no shaping of the hand grip. It is therefore even more important that the correct position should be sought out and adopted. A simple routine to establish the right position is worth pursuing to begin with, thereafter it should soon be assumed automatically every time you shoot (see photos 74-78).

Hold the bow with the arm downwards and with the string uppermost. Then to make sure that the hand is correctly positioned, first extend your thumb along the centre of the face of the bow – this will ensure that your fingers are neither too far round the hand grip, nor insufficiently so – then close your thumb round the hand grip. Do not grip the bow tightly, nor use too feeble a grasp, a controlled grip without tension is ideal. Now raise your bow arm to shoulder level with the bow horizontal to the ground, then turn your hand from the wrist so that the bow is exactly vertical. Do not twist your arm. If this is done properly the elbow of your bow arm will point outwards and not downwards. Flex your elbow joint slightly so that your arm gently curves away from the string. If there is a gap between the string and your arm then a good position has been achieved. There is a sound reason for this which relates to the necessity of allowing the bow string free passage once it has been released. If attention is not paid to the position of the bow arm as we have described it, undue tension in the arm can produce a sideways jerking of the bow, and there is the danger of the string fouling the sleeve or arm, throwing the arrow off course. Do not, therefore, lock the elbow of your bow arm.

The bow should be held as we have described it throughout shooting; too tight a grip can cause bad shooting. Additionally remember that the bow must remain vertical. A bow canted to left or right, even slightly, will throw arrows to right or left respectively. When the bow is under tension, i.e. at full draw, the pressure exerted by the bow hand must be evenly distributed. This is the reason why correct positioning of your bow hand is important. Extra pressure to the right or left on the bow handle, or too much pressure at the base of your hand, will result in arrows going off course.

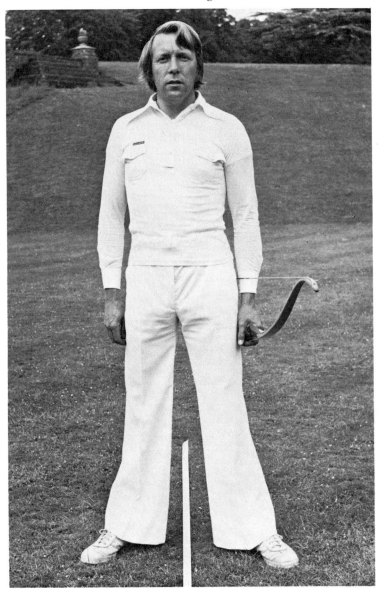

74. All movement from now on should be only from the upper part of the body and the arms.

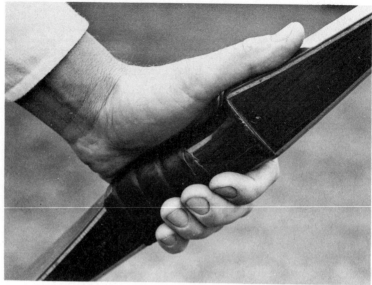

75. A useful method of positioning the hand correctly.

76. Now grasp the bow with a positive but not too strong a grip.

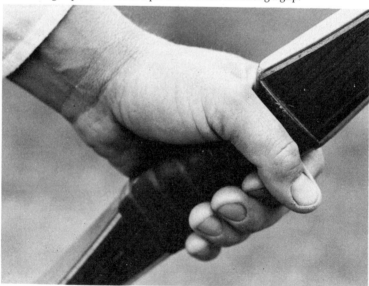

77. Raising the bow to shoulder level.

Over a century ago the art of archery was closely examined by
Horace Ford, who held the British Championship for twelve
years, an unbeaten record, and his logical and scientific approach

131

78. Turning the bow to the vertical position which can be difficult to get exactly right the first time.

made a significant contribution to the way in which shooting techniques have evolved ever since. He maintained that archery required 'both physical powers and mental study' a theme which, by now, should have impressed any newcomer to the sport, and which is clearly recognized by those with a little more experience in shooting. Accordingly it is a good idea to rehearse all the practical matters of archery by not only performing them physically but also by running through each aspect as a mental exercise. To start, take up the stance as we have described it and recall some of the essential preliminaries which govern the way an archer must stand to produce the best results. Ford summarized these essentials by saying that 'an archer's general position, to be a good one, must be possessed of three qualities – namely, firmness, elasticity and grace; firmness to resist the force, pressure and recoil of the bow; elasticity, to give free play to the muscles; and grace to render the shooter and his performance an agreeable object to the eye of the spectator'. We would add that an equally critical quality, which Ford omitted, was that of consistency, the fact that it is essential to assume the same position every time you shoot, achieve that and you have laid the soundest foundation for good shooting.

9

NOCKING AND DRAWING

According to Roger Ascham, the father of archery, 'To nock well is the easiest point of all', but like everything else in this study, it is best to carry out this simple task in a regular fashion. There are several ways in which this can be performed, and it matters little which method is employed so long as the same one is used all the time, and provided that certain matters are checked in the process.

To nock an arrow merely means to place it in position on the string, and when this is done it is essential that the arrow is pushed gently but firmly right home on the nocking point, and once in position it should remain there by the snugness of its fit. The second important matter to be checked is the position of the arrow on the string. This must be exactly at right-angles to the string and in just the same position every time nocking takes place. The slot of the nock on the end of the arrow bisects its diameter, and the three feathers are arranged at intervals of 120 °. One of these, called the cock feather, is set at right-angles to the slot and it is important to verify that the cock feather is in the correct position when the arrow is nocked. To enable the fletchings to clear the bow completely on release the cock feather should stand at right-angles away from the bow. The final point to be confirmed whilst nocking takes place is to see that the bracing height remains constant. To check this some archers find it convenient to paint cresting on their arrows at a position to correspond with the correct bracing height for the bow they are

135

79. The cock feather, which is set at right-angles to the arrow shaft, should point away from the bow. Note the nocking point on the string.

using, others use a gauge or tape measure for this purpose. Whatever the choice the essential thing is to make some provision for a simple and quickly applied method to confirm this vital measurement.

The correct method of nocking an arrow is the method that you find most convenient and comfortable, and the two most generally used ways of nocking are as follows. In the first the bow is held horizontally in front of the body at about waist level with the string towards you. Take an arrow between thumb and forefinger of the right hand, remove it from the quiver or ground

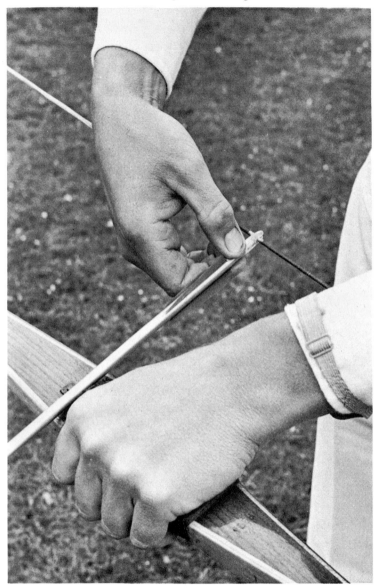

80. The first method of nocking the arrow.

quiver, and lay it across the bow against the arrow rest. Making sure that the cock feather is uppermost, draw the arrow back and carefully engage the nock with the nocking point of the string. If a 'clicker' is fitted to the bow then the arrow has to be first gently inserted under the sprung portion of the clicker before it is drawn back and engaged with the string. A modification of this method of nocking involves the arrow being slipped between string and bow, holding the nock between first and second fingers and bringing it back on to the string while the thumb is held behind the string.

The second method requires the bow to be held obliquely in front of the body with the string resting on the inside of the forearm. An arrow is drawn from the quiver with the right hand and held about half-way along its shaft, nock upwards. The arrow is then passed under the bow and the nock end is brought back towards the string and pushed home on the nocking point, again ensuring that the cock feather is correctly pointing away from the bow.

All is now ready for the fingers to be placed on the string, and we shall describe the most popular method of doing this by which a high standard of shooting can be maintained. In the process of drawing back a bow string the fingers of the drawing hand (the right in the case of a right-handed archer) act somewhat as a hook at the end of a lever. The form of that hook is important as not only does it have to allow the steadily increasing pressure of the drawn back bow string to be spread evenly, it also has to be able to be removed suddenly and cleanly to allow the string to be released sharply. The theoretical ideal is a mechanical lever or latch – but as this would destroy the whole principle of archery as we know it, (and would contravene Rule 103 (i)) we are stuck with a set of fingers of uneven length with which to do the best we can.

The most convenient method of drawing back a bow string used by modern archers is that which employs three fingers of the drawing hand hooked around the string. Place these three fingers in position on the string, one above and two below the arrow, so that the string lies across the crease of the first joints of the fingers, and the forefinger should lightly touch the arrow.

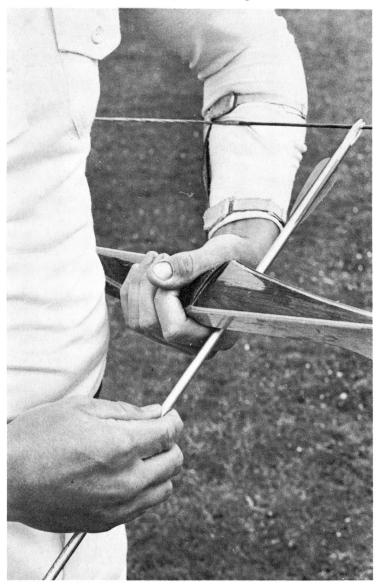

81. The second method of nocking the arrow.

The back of the hand must be flat, and the wrist must be straight. When the bow is drawn the angle formed by the string becomes more acute and there is a tendency for finger tips and arrow nock to become pinched together, besides being painful this deflects the arrow on release, so to compensate for this a slight gap is allowed between arrow and fingers. It is recommended that you leave a gap of about one eighth of an inch between your second finger and the arrow.

All the trouble taken to ensure that a correct initial position is assumed pays off in terms of a smooth, steady and comfortable draw. Now gently take up the tension of the string, adjusting your final hand position whilst under this slight tension. Keeping your fingers in place, let the string go back to its normal position and check that the arrow and drawing arm (or shaft arm) are exactly in line whether viewed from the side or from above. This

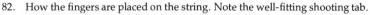

82.   How the fingers are placed on the string. Note the well-fitting shooting tab.

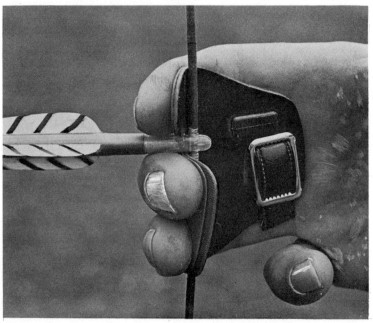

83. The Preparation Line.

84.   The Preparation Position or addressing the target.

is known as the Preparation Line, and although this will not be completely maintained once the bow is at full draw, the relationship between the two hands achieved at this stage is important, as when the bow is drawn both hands move together, though of course in opposite directions.

The proper shooting of one arrow into a target repeated over and over again is what we are aiming for, and so far our attention has been concentrated on what happens preparatory to releasing that one arrow. It is now time to begin thinking of bridging the gap between shooting line and target in a practical fashion. When you are confident that everything so far is as it should be, and this is where a rapid mental calculation is made of all the points you should have observed up to now, then and only then, clear your mind of extraneous thoughts and with body poised, not tense, and above all comfortable, turn your head towards the target and focus your gaze on it. You are now in what is described as the Preparation Position, known alternatively as 'addressing the target'.

Before we proceed to the all-important drawing of the arrow it may prove helpful to beginners to carry out some preliminary loosing practice to help them appreciate the operation of shooting without the effort of drawing the bow fully. It is a good idea to shoot some arrows into the ground a few yards away by the employment of a limited draw. Do this by drawing the bow back a short distance, six or eight inches will suffice, pause for a moment, then draw back another inch or so at the same time straightening the fingers of the shaft hand. This is the 'loose' and when you have got the hang of it, you will have some idea of the movement that is necessary to loose an arrow at full draw. Two simultaneous movements are involved; straightening the fingers, and moving the hand backwards continuing the direction of the Preparation Line. When the arrow is released, pause, keep the bow still and do not move the drawing hand for a few moments. Loose a few arrows in this fashion until you become used to the feel of it.

From the Preparation Position it is now time to come to full draw. During this action you should breathe normally and avoid

85.   Shooting a few arrows into the ground to get the feel of the loose.

Nocking and Drawing

taking a deep breath whilst drawing the bow. There are several ways in which the full draw position can be attained, and the one which is most generally used is as follows. It is best done with the two hands pushing and pulling respectively, extending the bow and string, at the same time bringing the bow to a vertical position with bow arm fully extended, and drawing back the shaft arm until the first finger touches just below the jaw. The Preparation Line, which involves keeping arrow and shaft arm in a straight line, should be maintained as far as possible throughout the draw as well as in the final position at full draw. The action is not performed solely with your fingers and arms. It should feel as though your shoulder muscles, right across the back, are doing the work, and that they are using your arms and fingers as levers and hooks, until your shoulder blades come

86.   The first method of drawing.

145

87. The string should lightly touch chin and nose at the full draw position.

together. The whole action of drawing must be done smoothly and fairly smartly, without jerking.

Ideally at full draw the string should just touch the centre of your nose and chin, but on no account must it touch your chest. This is the recommended arrangement, and if there is any difficulty in getting it right, a slight tilting forward of the head may be the answer. During the whole sequence of drawing the body position must remain static and the shoulders should be kept level. The point to which the forefinger of the shaft hand is drawn underneath the centre of the chin is known as the Anchor Point, and it is to this spot that the arrow must be drawn precisely each time a shot is made. This will bring the Line of Sight and the Line of Flight into their correct relationship. To maintain the same vertical distance between Anchor Point, string and eye, is most important, for by varying this distance, the angle between the

146

Nocking and Drawing

Line of Sight and the Line of Flight is altered, consistency is lost, and each successive shot will not exactly follow its predecessor.

A second method of drawing consists of raising the bow whilst maintaining the Preparation Line until the bow hand is approximately level with the top of the head, the upper part of the bow arm being in the full draw position. The shaft hand should be about six inches clear of the face and at right-angles to the string, with the nock of the arrow about level with the mouth. Bring the bow hand down, at the same time extending the bow to full draw making sure that the string is brought back to touch chin and nose as before.

88.   The second method of drawing.

This method of drawing has a special application in that it is suited for disabled archers confined to wheelchairs, who find that they cannot easily manage the first method described. It is also useful as an alternative for those who have difficulties in overcoming excessive body movement when drawing, or who shove the shoulder of the bow arm forward on this action, and in this connection you will recall that we emphasized earlier the fact that the body position must remain static and the shoulders horizontal when a bow is drawn.

A third method of drawing is one that is more easily mastered by more experienced archers. It has an advantage in that minimal movement is required, but unlike the methods already described

89. The third method of drawing.

90. No matter what method of draw is used the final position at full draw must
be consistent.

it involves some slight movement of the body, which if not
recovered properly can throw the arrow off line. The method

149

starts with the bow held upright with the bow arm slightly bent. Draw back the string, at the same time pushing the bow forward to full draw position.

No matter what method is used the final full draw position that is assumed must be consistent. There are several points to remember. All movement must be smooth and under control, not too fast nor too slow. The bow arm should be slightly flexed with the elbow pointing outwards and not downwards. Try to achieve controlled relaxation, the elbow must not be locked in a rigid position, and the wrist and shoulders should not be taut. The positioning of the bow and arrow in relation to the shaft arm describes an imaginary line, sometimes described as the Draw Force Line, and ideally this is where the elbow, the nock of the arrow and the point at which the bow hand is taking the weight of the bow, form a straight line.

It may be easier for beginners to practise drawing the bow without an arrow to get the feel of what is, to most, an unaccustomed movement. Do not, however, release the string without an arrow in the bow, as a 'dry release' as this is called, can be harmful to the bow.

Drawing is the beginning of the sequence of shooting. From the moment the archer begins this movement there is only one escape from conscious errors. It happens, occasionally, even with champions, that a slight fault in drawing back the arrow, which would mar an otherwise perfect shot, is realized in time. Then the archer must let down his bow, replace the arrow in the quiver, take up the Preparation Position anew, clear his mind and start again. Try to discipline yourself mentally to check all the finer points of the act of shooting as the action unfolds; it will very soon become relatively automatic. If there appears to be something not quite right, start again and give yourself time to think of what might have gone wrong, and correct it the second time. Develop your own shooting rhythm by perfecting each individual stage of the whole sequence, linking them together in a pattern which can be repeated consistently, and the accuracy and certainty of hitting the target will follow.

10

HOLDING

Once the bow has been fully drawn, there is a pause during which the aim is fixed. It is also a convenient moment for the archer to make a rapid assessment of the correctness of every point which has to be observed to enable him to successfully accomplish the task ahead.

This is, in many ways, the most critical part of the whole sequence of shooting. It marks the accumulation of effort and skill which forms the basis for the all-important release of the arrow. Therefore, if by now everything is not right, there is every possibility, other than by fluke, of the shot being less than perfect. Do not be too anxious to loose the arrow, it is at this moment of pause, when the bow is held at full draw, that a number of faults may be recognized. It is much easier to see many of these faults in others, and to get someone, who knows what to look for of course, to watch your shooting, can be a great advantage. As an alternative to persuading someone to observe this critical stage, the beginner is recommended to get the feel of the final pose at full draw, preferably with dummy equipment, in front of a mirror. This is an ideal procedure to check your own stance, head and arm positions, shoulders and so on.

In many ways the concentration required at this point requires a special effort of mental discipline. In fact by studying archers who are consistently good shots, one can observe a deliberate attempt to achieve complete concentration at this moment, to the exclusion of all outside distractions. To cultivate the habit of making a mental assessment of your own performance is not only an advantage to your shooting it is also an excellent mental exercise.

Let us repeat the most important matters to watch for and to think over during the pause. The shaft arm and the arrow must still be in line, remember the Preparation Line, and any tendency to raise or drop the elbow must be checked. The distance the arrow is drawn back must be constant and this can only be achieved after you have gained confidence, through practice, in performing one or two essential matters, and after you are able to control a complexity of variables which govern this distance of draw. To explain further: the bow arm has to be extended forward, slightly flexed remember, to exactly the same distance every time an arrow is drawn and when you contemplate on the variety of movements that an arm can perform, and the number of positions it can assume, with hinge joints, ball and socket joints, flexible tendons, muscles and so on, you will realize the necessity of the precise control that must be cultivated in order to reach out in space to just the same spot over and over again. Once the shaft arm has been drawn back to anchor at a precise location, no movement forward or backward of either hand must be allowed.

The position of the arrow point in relation to the eye must remain constant, both vertically and horizontally, and the importance of this geometry was explained in our discussion of the theory of aiming. Any vertical alteration in the distance between the eye and the position of the Anchor Point, even a fraction of an inch, will be multiplied by the time the arrow reaches its destination. Therefore such matters as tilting the head or opening the mouth must be avoided.

We have already commented on the fact that the hands must not move forward or backward, now check that they are balanced, that is to say they must not be twisted in relationship to each other. The shaft hand should remain flat, the fingers should be in line and not slanted. Make sure that the pressure on the bow handle is evenly distributed and that this is maintained throughout shooting, above all do not grip the bow tightly. It is the bow

91. Taking aim at the full draw position.

that is held in balance and not the arrow. Watch the position of the bow itself, it should neither be canted to left or right, nor tilted backwards or forwards, but should remain quite vertical.

During this brief interval under no circumstances must the arms, chest and shoulders be allowed to sag, which can produce the fault known as 'creeping'. In this the arrow imperceptibly creeps forward shortening the effective draw length, whilst the archer, blissfully unaware of what is happening, experiences disappointment at another poor shot and bewilderment as to its cause. It is simply explained, the power of the bow diminishes in proportion to the reduction of draw length, and therefore if creeping is allowed to take place the accuracy of successive shots is prejudiced by variable thrusts at release.

Many inexperienced archers have suffered the irritation of the arrow falling off the arrow shelf once the bow has been drawn. This can be caused if the drawn arrow is pinched between the fingers, or if the shaft hand and bow hand are out of line or twisted in relationship to each other. If a clicker is used the arrow is held back and cannot fall off the arrow shelf, but opposed to this advantage, if faults are present such as those that we have described, they are prevented from being revealed by the use of this device. Therefore it is wise not to use a clicker until you are certain that you have mastered hand and finger positions and that you have eliminated any possibility of this fault occurring.

We have spoken about the pattern of shooting evolving as a personal rhythm, each separate action of body and mind being gradually linked together to form a complete sequence, that of shooting an arrow. It is not a bad idea to constantly remind yourself of this theme and to persist in the search for the best possible rhythm for you alone. Archery is not a team sport in the sense that you require a partner or other members of a team with whom you join in action, it is uniquely individual, to the extent that you can indulge in creating your own personalized pattern of shooting. However, there must be some limits to individualism, and one such matter is the length of time a bow is held at full draw in the aiming position. This varies according to the archer, some take what appears to be a considerable length of time before finally loosing the arrow, whereas others are brief and dismiss their arrows as though they are glad to be done with them. When shooting a round, under the rules of G.N.A.S. or F.I.T.A., a limit of 2½ minutes is allowed for an archer to shoot three arrows from the moment he steps on to the shooting line. More than ample time, in fact, for anyone to carry out all that is necessary without haste.

In chapter six we described the normal method of aiming used when shooting arrows from a bow, it is now time to put this into practice. However for those who have learnt the rudiments of archery and who have started to shoot, there is often a temptation to get arrows in the general direction of the target without carefully considering the theoretical aspects of aiming. Consequently many beginners do not understand fully the principles involved, with a result that they are disappointed in their early endeavours to hit the target.

92. In this study the archer has adopted an alternative means of locating a consistent anchor point.

The basic principle to remember each time a correction of aim is taken is that what really happens is an adjustment to the elevation of the arrow. The best method of making that adjustment is by a slight movement of the body from the waist, without moving hips or legs, and without spoiling the relationship of all the other positions which you have so carefully perfected beforehand. Once the aim is set it is visually held on the target preparatory to the loose, and this moment can cause problems for some archers. It is wise to hold the aim just long enough to be sure that all is well, but lack of certainty in this connection may lead to an over-long hold or, conversely, insufficient time may be spent through impatience or over-confidence.

So long as the whole sequence is controlled by conscious effort no problems arise that cannot easily be settled. However once the process of shooting starts to become an automatic order of events, without conscious effort, the eye is allowed to take over during the pause and a conditioned reflex develops. The muscular mechanism for releasing the arrow is tripped by the eye, and the arrow is discharged prematurely. It is found that it is impossible to hold the sight on the right spot on the target, and attempts to visually bring it into position only produce a 'freezing' of the aim.

Much has been written about this *maladie de la carte*, and many theories have been advanced as to its cause and cure. It has been searchingly discussed by medical experts, dismissed casually and sometimes lightheartedly by victims and observers alike, and occasionally dismally accepted as inevitable and incurable. It has caught the attention of every modern writer on archery shooting techniques and it has been variously called Target Shyness, Gold Shyness, Target Panic, Archer's Paralysis, Freezing and many other descriptive and uncomplimentary names. The archer afflicted will find it all too easy to recognize, although the beginner can take heart as it seems to affect only those who have reached a reasonably proficient standard of shooting. Let us consider what causes this inability to hold the aim.

The process of reasoning by which psychologists explain the

93. A target's eye view of an arrow held at full draw whilst aiming takes place. Note the slight curve in the bow arm away from the string.

condition is profound; instead of discussing these complexities let us examine some of the practical factors which are known to encourage and aggravate the situation. These can be grouped as influences which interfere with the normal rhythm of shooting. We have already explained that this rhythm is highly individual and that it has to be evolved gradually. This is the reason why a novice, not having produced such a pattern of his own, rarely experiences the freezing effect of these influences. The use of wrong muscular tensions through being overbowed is a common factor, another is fatigue. The influence of anxiety or tension felt in competition, or worry that the next shot will be a bad one, lack of adequate powers of concentration, distractions of various kinds – all these can contribute to the utter breakdown of the fractional moment between aiming and loosing. To summarily deal with the causes of this problem as we have done, does not do justice to the enormous amount of analysis and study of it contributed by specialists of medicine and toxophily over the years. However it is our intention to provide the means of recognition and, what will be more comforting, suggest a cure.

In the first place an archer who experiences freezing for the first time must stop and decide on the course he must take – trying harder merely aggravates the problem. One thing he can be absolutely certain of is that the situation is not hopeless! Usually it is not enough to remove the cause, even if it has been identified as still being present; it is necessary to neutralize its effect. Much has been said about the rhythm of shooting which has been consciously achieved. It is the part of the rhythm between aiming and loosing which has become automatic that we are attempting to bring into line as part of this conscious performance. Alter this and the fault will be neutralized. Possibly the cure sounds too easy, there is no guarantee that it will be permanent, but as there are countless variations of change which can be applied, any number of cures can be effected.

Any positive alteration will usually work, adopting a different form of shooting, using alternative methods of sighting, chang-ing a bead sight to a ring sight, altering the sighting mark on the target to a spot other than the gold, using both eyes if you have begun to use one, and a drastic alteration, changing from right-handed shooting to left-handed or vice versa. Some authorities recommend the introduction of an intermediate stage of shooting between aiming and loosing, described as 'balance', and many archers find the solution in the use of a clicker. Numerous other changes work equally well, but it is important to persevere with whatever new arrangement is chosen, remembering that it is up to the archer concerned to make the change work for him as no alteration can automatically eliminate this very common malady.

All these matters may seem to be a lengthy catalogue of 'remember this' and 'don't forget that', but they are important, and each point, if it is not done properly, will produce a shooting error. These are essential aspects of technique which are worth studying, because once the arrow has left the bow its direction is predetermined, and the result of bad technique can never be changed. Far better to ensure that, by developing a good technique, you are doing everything possible to shoot the arrow as accurately as it can be shot. The course of the arrow depends entirely on the climax of physical control on release. Thus any factor which interferes with the proper management of the pause should be thoroughly investigated and dealt with. So long as the whole sequence is controlled by conscious effort no problems arise. Good scores, and personal satisfaction, begin with careful attention to these matters.

11

THE LOOSE

The loose is the most critical of all the points of archery, and extra effort in the management of finger movements in the early days will prove beneficial as you become more skilled. Whereas with some application a novice can soon manage to perform this action after a fashion, the perfecting of a correct loosing motion is not easy to acquire and takes considerable practice. In fact the secret of archery is the rehearsing of the loose and attempting to perfect it, for he who can loose without fault holds the key to perfect archery. The action required is simple enough; once the arrow, bow and string are positioned at full draw in exactly the right alignment towards the mark, all the stored energy in the bow must be suddenly released so that it can propel the arrow to its required destination. This works extremely well – if none of the positioning is disturbed.

Let us examine again the moment before the loose. The string is held back by half-bent fingers in an unnatural tension, the bow is held forward in space to just the right distance, and the eye is momentarily mesmerized by a good aim on the target. Alter one of these factors by just a fraction and the shot is spoiled. There are many other considerations which, once settled, must not be altered. Imagine that the archer stands firm, and then suddenly his fingers holding the string are not there, and you have a reasonably good idea of the sought-after action of loosing. The string must not slip gradually off the fingers, neither must they be snatched off the string; the loose must be smooth and easy, without any jerk.

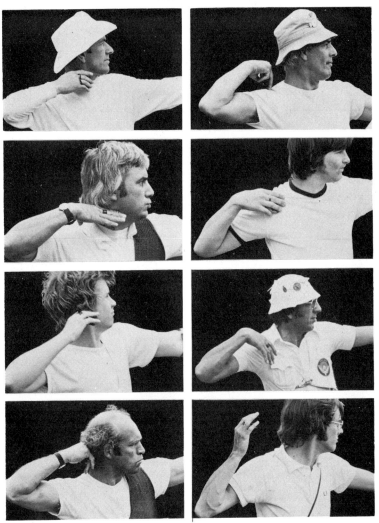

94. A series of action studies showing variations in the backward movement of the shaft hand after the loose.

The recommended method of achieving a good loose consists of a series of carefully controlled simultaneous movements. The shaft arm, holding back the arrow, should be relaxed and held in position by the back muscles. If a little extra muscular effort is exerted from the back this will result in the arm being moved slightly back in the direction of the Draw Force Line. This results in the string being pressed back a little harder on to the chin. At the same moment the fingers holding the string should be straightened, and the arrow leaves the bow. These movements, which are hardly perceptible to the observer, must be exactly co-ordinated. If all this occurs correctly, no change in the string position results up to its final release, and the loose is clean and sharp. The fingers should be relaxed and not too stiff or taut when they are straightened, and it is most important that all three fingers should quit the string simultaneously.

Because of the released tension of the drawn bow, the drawing hand will continue to move backwards, close to the neck. Often this backward movement is continued for an inch or so, or even further, but provided a clean loose is achieved there is no harm in this. However, it is important to keep the hand from turning until after the loose has been completed. Wrist and hand are relaxed, and this relaxation will be apparent once the string is free of the fingers.

The tendency to allow the arrow to creep forward momentarily before the loose, which we discussed earlier, must be carefully checked. Remember that the arrow must remain at exactly the same draw length until the actual moment of release. Resist the temptation to look at the pile of the arrow at full draw to see whether it has been drawn back far enough, otherwise your eyes will have to change focus from their concentration on the aim on the target. The use of the clicker has helped to eliminate this problem with some archers, but it is far better to perfect a satisfactory loose without such aids.

A method which has proved useful in practising the loose is what is called 'blind loosing'. Stand close to a target, say two yards or so away, and with your eyes closed go through the whole sequence of drawing and loosing. Without any outside distractions you can concentrate more deeply on all the things that should be done, and a good clean loose will soon be recognized by the feel of the action. This also eliminates the additional mental and physical activities needed for aiming, and you can, therefore, concentrate on the all-important moment of loose. If you decide to indulge in blind loosing remember two things, the eyes should be closed for a period of time, not just for a moment while the action takes place, and above all ask a friend to supervise this activity from the aspect of safety.

When the arrow is loosed the released tension tends to allow both arms and the bow to move out of their proper positions. The bow hand and arm should remain exactly in the position they were in the aim, and the shaft arm and hand should move back only in the direction of the Draw Force Line. Some archers use a very light grip on the bow, and to prevent it from springing from the hand they use some form of simple harness known usually as a bow sling. There is no harm in letting the bow move freely at this stage, so long as the released string does not strike the bracer or arm. Remain perfectly still, with hands, arms and body in just the same position as when the loose was performed until the arrow has found its mark. Under no circumstances must you watch the flight of the arrow, and your visual aim on the target must be maintained. This passive part of the shooting sequence is known as the Follow Through. Lack of control at this stage can cause trouble. If, for example, your hands fall away before the arrow reaches the target there is a tendency for them to start moving at or even before the moment of loosing. The practice of a Follow Through for each arrow shot ensures that the complete rhythm of shooting is not disturbed or abruptly curtailed. It is after this that you can relax, consider the success or otherwise of your shot, mentally correct any errors, clear your mind and prepare for the next arrow.

If you have persevered so far and have performed everything as you should have done, you should very soon experience a positive control over the arrows you are shooting. When an arrow is projected from a bow its direction is the result of a carefully orchestrated shooting sequence over which only the archer has control. This control can be automatically programmed or it can be the result of conscious effort. There is, therefore, a difference between a purely mechanical shooting technique

163

95. The use of a bow sling.

carried out as a routine, done without thinking, and a technique of which every second is being masterminded by a continuous and conscious mental process. The detailed process of shooting a bow and arrow is rarely the same for two days running, minor changes have to be made to accommodate variations in weather, environmental differences, a kaleidoscope of emotions, and many other influential factors, and the best judge of what those changes should be is the archer himself. Once shooting has been allowed to become totally automatic the adaptability of the process is reduced, the performance suffers, and the archer experiences a feeling of despondency which accompanies failure without apparent cause.

To master the loose is the most difficult matter of all, yet once you get the hang of it, like riding a bicycle, it is something never forgotten. You should be aware of what is happening to each end of six arrows you shoot, and if these arrows all finish up in the target – good; if they finish up close together in the target – excellent! It really matters more to begin with that your arrows are closely grouped than the position of that grouping on the target. A good group is a clear indicator that you are shooting consistently. Accuracy, in the sense that you are hitting the centre of the target, can be contrived by adjustment of the sight, then the group is moved rather than the position of one arrow. When you are confident that you can reasonably group your arrows in the central area of the target, then move the target back progressively ten yards or so at a time until you reach one of the normal middle distance ranges used for competitive shooting. However, do not be too anxious to shoot the extreme distances; to begin with polish up your performance at the lesser distances. If you find that a practice session does not show the improvement for which you hoped, first, have patience; second, stop shooting, relax and think through the shooting sequence, recalling its every aspect in the correct order; third, start again and amend only one item at a time as necessary until improvement occurs.

12

CORRECTING FAULTS

The recognition of faults, their analysis and correction has occupied a great deal of space in the textbooks of archery over the years, and advice as to how one should approach the practical aspect of shooting invariably includes warnings of the pitfalls likely to be met. The beginner expects to make initial mistakes, although it is logical to assume that by having the proper instruction and following it precisely, it should lead to the elimination of errors at the outset. However it is rare for anyone to become so proficient that he is faultless, even with the help of the up-to-date coaching methods that are used today. The correction of faults in archery is a constant process and this applies equally to beginners and the most skilled archers. It is commonplace for a fault to develop quite suddenly and unbeknown to the archer, even though he may have years of experience of first class shooting to his credit. Some of the results of faulty performance are sadly too obvious to the archer and spectator alike, when for instance the shots miss the target completely, other manifestations of bad shooting are not so obvious and can bring disappointment and bewilderment to the shooter, particularly when he is not aware of their cause.

Everyone on the shooting line at sometime or another realizes that something is wrong, or feels that the rhythm of shooting is momentarily out of tune, and is vaguely aware that he or she is doing something incorrectly. Quite often the feeling is dismissed and shooting continues, uninterrupted by any self-analysis,

96.   A good group of arrows high on the target.

advice from others, or correction, or very likely because time presses and the round must be finished. The damage has been done. A fault has crept in and if something is not done about it it will return and very soon it will begin to produce a deterioration in shooting. Far better to sacrifice the last dozen or so arrows in a round, and devote a little time to the very necessary labours of fault correction. It is not a disagreeable task – in fact it becomes

167

personally satisfying to identify the most insignificant fault, and an individual triumph when it is conquered. It is only by a deliberate and methodical process of deduction that one can identify just what is wrong.

Once the whole sequence of shooting one arrow is mastered, it is then necessary to do everything in exactly the same way for each subsequent shot. This need for consistency in every movement is something which we have repeated more than once, but it can only be achieved by consciously thinking through the sequence of shooting for each individual arrow. After considerable practice the process becomes nearly automatic and when this stage is reached it is well to remember that not only must you think of what you are doing, but you must also consider whether what you are doing is right! Combined with this mental process you have to constantly monitor your performance, particularly in so far as the end result is concerned. In other words the destination of each arrow must be considered in relation to the previous one. Thus the combination of 'what did I

97.   The tendency to allow the arms to collapse forward can produce low shots.

168

do?' and 'did I do it correctly?', together with a mental record of where the arrow finished, will form an analysis of your own shooting technique and performance and a basis for correction if necessary – or a signal to repeat the sequence exactly, if everything was as it should have been.

Apart from the mental appraisal which will often reveal a fault, it is sometimes helpful to persuade a friend to watch every movement and to point out the obvious mistakes. It is easy to see certain defects in other people's shooting, although the archer concerned may be unaware of their existence. However, when shooting a round under G.N.A.S. rules no criticism or advice can be given to an archer once he is on the shooting line. [Rule 104 (j)]. It is easier to pinpoint a fault if at least six arrows, one end, are considered, and it is of little use isolating the performance of any one arrow. The better the arrows are grouped on the target the easier it is to correct their collective position, and this applies, to a large extent, if the arrows are in a good group on the ground.

A most important approach to the problem of faulty shooting is that one cannot expect to satisfactorily resolve problems which occur unless sufficient knowledge has been accumulated to begin with. For example it is one thing to recognize that you are doing something badly, but another to know what error in shooting is produced by that particular fault. Conversely having isolated an error it is just as important to identify its cause as to recognize its character.

Even Olympic and World Champions have never been able to hit the target in exactly the same spot with every arrow for the duration of a round, so, if we discount adverse weather conditions, there must be at least one other factor which disturbs the perfect sequence of shooting. In general the majority of faults can be attributed to bad individual technique. Among such faults may be those that are essentially physical (wrong body, arm and hand positions, incorrect movements and so on), some which relate to timing, and others which are psychological. Outside distractions such as fatigue, or even anger and frustration, are other causes which result in bad technique, which in turn spoils an otherwise good shot. Other causes of incorrect shooting can be

169

98. Another cause of low arrows is dropping the bow arm on release.

identified as technical faults, or those which include faulty or incorrect equipment.

Imagine for a moment that the target is represented by a clock face, the numerals marking sectors of 30 °, and if we divide each of those sectors by the five colour rings the whole area of the target face is divided into sixty imaginary but easily identifiable sections. This is a useful aid in describing positions of any arrow on the target. Every fault in archery amounts to the same thing – the fact that the arrow does not reach the exact spot on the target that was planned. Some shots are high, some are low, some left or right of the sought-after central spot. Others, of course, miss altogether but it matters where they miss, one side or the other or high or low. Let us examine some of the most common faults which can spoil what may have been otherwise satisfactory shooting. The four basic results of inaccurate shooting are:

170

Correcting Faults

1. Shooting high, 11 to 1 o'clock, or over.
2. Shooting low, 5 to 6 o'clock, or under (see photos 97, 98).
3. Shooting to the right, 2 to 4 o'clock, or missing right.
4. Shooting to the left, 8 to 10 o'clock, or missing left.

The following permutations can be added to the above; high-right, 1 to 2 o'clock; low-right, 4 to 5 o'clock; low-left, 7 to 8 o'clock; and high-left, 10 to 11 o'clock. The nearer the arrows are to the centre the less the effective degree of fault, thus a gold at 12 o'clock would score the same as a gold at 6 o'clock, and if this particular pattern continued at one of the longer distances, the shooting would be of a very high standard. Therefore we have to take into consideration the distance of shooting and exactly where on the target the arrows fall before we can classify the shot as a faulty one. However at any distance the appearance of a 'scatter', where arrows have struck haphazardly on the target and in the ground, indicates that a number of faults may be present. In addition, even if arrows are grouped well, but are badly placed on the target, this can be the result of more than one fault in shooting. It is therefore necessary to apply the principle of elimination, dealing with one possibility at a time until the error is rectified.

In general errors can be grouped under two main characteristics, errors in the vertical plane and errors in the horizontal plane. Let us first discuss the causes of vertical errors which can be assigned entirely to faulty equipment. Several minor mishaps can produce shooting errors such as the sight slipping up and down the track, bent arrows, slight expansion or stretching of the string which can let the bow down, alteration in the bracing height, or the centre serving on the string may have slipped, or changing the position of the nocking point. Several other matters of this nature can occur and the cure is obvious – make sure that your equipment is in good order every time you use it, and throughout shooting carry out periodic checks to see that these items are as they should be.

Shooting high can result from over-drawing, which in turn may be due to an incorrect stance. Associated with this is the over-drawing which results from using arrows which are too long, or re-locating the Anchor Point further back along the jaw, thus drawing the arrow back too far. The arrow must remain steady in line, and any movement which pushes the forward end up or the rear end down produces a high shot. For example, dropping the shaft hand can cause this, or opening the mouth has the same effect. Pinching the arrow can also lift it off the arrow-rest, or the arrow can be put off line by raising the bow hand.

The moment of release is all-important and a bad loose can produce any amount of errors. A sharpened loose, or a snatched loose performed in an inconsistent manner, usually sends an arrow flying higher than intended. Care must be taken to release the string with all your fingers at the same time. If the loose is achieved by letting the fingers lag behind each other the arrow will not fly as it should. If the third finger looses first, the arrow will fly higher. There should be no space between fingers and chin and some archers find the use of a 'kisser', which usually consists of a small rubber disc attached to the string, helpful in finding the right location. The kisser must not exceed 1 cm in width. [Rule 103 (e)].

99. A common fault is holding the shaft arm too high at full draw.

Correcting Faults

Improper control of the bow can produce inaccurate shooting. A high shot will be the result if the bow is pushed forward at the moment of loosing. If the bow is tilted backwards, possibly caused by undue pressure below the centre of the pressure point of the hand on the bow, or 'heeling', a high shot will result. Additionally, arrows will go high if the body is bent backwards, or if the bow hand is turned upwards.

Many of the faults which produce low flying arrows are the opposite of those which caused high shots. A very common cause is under-drawing, which can be the result of several faults. A bow arm which imperceptibly sags or collapses from holding the aim too long will allow the arrow to creep forward, which causes loss of power in the bow and prevents the spine of the arrow from reacting properly. The re-location of the Anchor Point forward, thus producing an under-drawn arrow, is another matter which must be avoided.

Control of the bow is again important if low arrows are to be avoided. If excess pressure is applied above the centre of the pressure point of the hand on the bow, called 'topping', then low shots will result. Another common cause of low flying arrows is dropping the bow hand on release, this in turn may be due to the drawing elbow being held too high. The loose can contribute to low arrows in the opposite way to that which we described as producing high shots. If the forefinger is allowed to loose the string first, arrows will fly low.

The proper handling and control of the bow is vital if horizontal errors are to be avoided. First make sure that the bow is not low-strung, that is to say check that the bracing height is correct. There will be a tendency for arrows to fly to the left if the bow is held too tightly and if it is turned to the right in the hand. This is described as applying excessive torque. If the bow is tilted to the right (as the archer sees it) arrows will fly to the left. The string position must be controlled, it must always be released in the true Line of Flight. Discrepancies here can be the result of jerking the shaft hand away from the face on release (remember it must travel back in line, close to the neck), or re-location of the Anchor Point too far to the right. Another matter to watch for is keeping

100.   Horizontal errors — a group of arrows on the left of the target.

the string hand vertical, if it is tilted out of true it has the effect of producing a kink in the string, or 'dog-leg', thus disturbing the true direction of the string on release. Another cause of left flying arrows can be jerking the shaft hand away from the face on release. Interruption of the path of the released string can also produce the same bad fault, throwing it off line, and this can occur if it hits the bracer or fouls loose clothing. Arrows which are

101.   The results of good shooting.

allowed to creep will also tend to fly left as well as low.

The last of the common errors of shooting, shooting right, can be caused by the opposite of some of the faults which produced horizontal errors to the left. The handling and control of the bow is again important, a slackened grip or the application of torque in the opposite direction can cause arrows to fly to the right. Tilting the bow to the left (as the archer sees it), is another frequent cause of arrows flying to the right. A bad loose, such as not opening the fingers cleanly on release, can also contribute to this error. In addition make sure that the string is not held too deeply on the fingers.

The above series of faults in technique is by no means complete, what we have outlined are those which most generally appear. If the proper technique is not applied consistently, one or more of these faults can creep in, and each time this happens you must make the corrections immediately. Some of these faults are

175

easy to rectify, others take a little more time, particularly if they have been allowed to become a habit.

It must be emphasized that many archers make good scores by evolving their own minor points of technique, this is not a bad thing, provided that everything is consistently performed. However the routines which we have explained, if carried out diligently, can improve your shooting, but this must be accompanied by regular practice and a desire to better your previous performance. There is a great personal satisfaction in discovering that you can do better, but like all discoveries it is the result of a certain amount of perseverance. The more you persevere, the more you will improve, the more you improve the greater your enjoyment in shooting in a bow.

PART FOUR

Variety and Competition

13

VARIETY IN ARCHERY

Earlier in this book we referred to the fact that there were several forms of archery which could be pursued. We have concentrated on one of these, and the techniques for Target Archery which we have described are, with some modification, the basis for all forms of shooting. The principles which govern the operation of a bow are unchangeable, even in the most advanced equipment, and whereas the bow remains constant in its mechanical characteristics and the performance of the arrow conforms to unalterable rules of ballistics, the variable factor in archery, as we have endeavoured to point out, is the archer himself. In enjoying the bow and arrow in different ways, the archer has to change his technique to conform with contrasting forms of shooting and diverse arrangements of targets. Many of the alternative forms of archery have been handed down over the centuries and they are practised today with slight modifications, and the choice is widened by more recently devised alternative ways of shooting which conform to more modern trends. All these varieties of the way in which archery can be pursued have been carefully regularized, and separate rules for each of them have been included in G.N.A.S. *Rules of Shooting*.

Possibly the most popular form of shooting following Target Archery is Field Archery. This consists of shooting at special targets, either bold black and white circles, or animal figures with scoring zones superimposed on them, placed at a wide variety of distances in rough country. As an indication of the popularity of

179

102. Competitors at the William Somner Tournament, one of many such open meetings held throughout the season.

this form of shooting, led by the American example, there are a number of associations solely devoted to this activity, and since 1969 F.I.T.A. have sponsored World Field Archery Championships. Field Archery has its special rounds, two of which the Hunter and Field Rounds, being those recognized by F.I.T.A. and several others recognized by G.N.A.S. (*Rules* Part XII) According to the particular round there are different arrangements for placing targets of varying sizes at a planned series of distances. For example the Forester's Round consists of a total of fourteen targets; three having 24 inch diameter faces placed at distances of up to 70 yards, four 18 inch faces up to 50 yards, four 12 inch faces up to 40 yards and three of 6 inches diameter placed at up to 20 yards. Each target situation is chosen for its appropriateness, utilizing the terrain to the best advantage, high, low, across water, deep in undergrowth, in fact in every way that the ingenuity of the organizers can devise, so long as the rules are obeyed and that a clear shot can be obtained. Archers move round the course taking turns to shoot at each target from shooting posts at marked or unmarked distances, and scores are recorded by a Target Captain, whose responsibilities are similar to those he has in Target Archery.

There are separate classes for ladies, gentlemen and juniors, and three styles in which one can shoot dependant on the type of equipment used. In the Instinctive or Bare-bow class the bow must be free of any sights or marks which could be used for aiming and no field glasses or devices for estimating distances can be used. The Free-style class allows the use of sights, but field glasses and rangefinders are not permitted. Any arrows may be used except broadheads or arrows that may cause damage to the target faces and butts. A special form of arrow-point for Field Shooting is frequently used by enthusiasts, which is designed to be easily removed from tree trunks and similar objects if the target is missed. Longer fletchings than those used for target shooting are also popular and these are designed to give a steady and flat trajectory, although the cast of the bow is reduced slightly due to the extra drag which they cause, but these refinements are optional. In the Traditional class archers shoot

103. The completely different character of Field Archery appeals to a large number of archers who seek variety in their shooting.

under Bare-bow class rules with the important exception that wooden arrows must be used.

In Field Archery there are arrangements similar to those we met with in Target Archery for obtaining classifications according to proficiency, after the requisite qualifying scores have been made. The details of the regulations for securing titles of Grand Master Bowman (Field), Master Bowman (Field), and Class 1, 2 or 3 (Field) Archers, are laid down in Rule 367 (g).

As the terrain is likely to be uneven the formal stance that we took so much trouble to perfect as target archers, can be discarded, and the most convenient and stable position for shooting has to be found. This may be stooping, crouching, on a steep incline or even sitting, but the best has to be made of awkward situations, remembering that the principles of body,

182

arms, and bow relationship have to be maintained as far as possible. It is a comforting thought that the difficulties created by rough and uneven situations are just the same for everyone competing!

The method of shooting used for Field Archery is a matter for individual choice. In the Free-style class archers invariably take advantage of the fact that sights are allowed, and where distances are marked there is no problem in making the necessary aiming adjustments to those sights. However where the distances are unmarked it is a matter of judgement of distance and setting the sights to the range that is estimated. In the Bare-bow class, where no sighting devices are allowed, a widely used method of aiming

104. The Royal Company of Archers in Edinburgh shooting at the Clout.

is by utilizing the point of aim principle, which we described in chapter six, the only difference being that no separate device can be used as a personal sighting mark. Instead the archer chooses a mark, either on the target itself, or an imaginary spot in space which is a visually estimated distance from the target. With experience a field archer knows that if he aims at a spot so many inches or so many degrees away from the centre of the target, his arrow will reach the right mark. It will be seen that this method of aiming combines what could be called mental geometry and a sound judgement of distance. Either method is effective, the first depends on the use of sights set at actual or estimated ranges, and the second, known as the 'space-picture' method of aiming, requires precise judgement, visual accuracy and a lot of practice.

Purely instinctive shooting does not rely on any preconceived

105. Taking the scores at Clout Shooting. The radii of the different scoring rings are marked on a cord which is pivoted around the central flag.

106. Short powerful bows and very slim arrows are used in Flight Shooting.

pattern of sighting or theory of aiming, and some archers find that they can achieve reasonable accuracy just by pointing the arrow in the right direction and loosing it. In taking aim with the tip of the arrow it is helpful if the view is taken, as far as possible, along the length of the arrow, and to facilitate this a higher Anchor Point is normally used. The arrow is drawn back to the side of the face and an Anchor Point is chosen which must be the same spot every time an arrow is drawn. Adjustment to the eye position, to get it closer to the arrow, can be made by leaning the head forward slightly to one side and forward so that you have an even more direct view along the shaft. Before you experiment with any of these styles remember that it is still absolutely necessary to maintain consistency in shooting, in fact with Field Archery some of the order and regularity of the target range is absent, and it requires a keener discipline to maintain a consistent pattern of technique.

Field Archery is a sophisticated adaptation of practice for hunting with the bow and in its present form it can be said to have descended from the practice of Rovers, in which groups of archers roved through the woods and fields picking out as a target any suitable mark, such as a log or mound. In seventeenth-century England as the sport became more popular it began to be played on a course with permanent marks, such as existed over Finsbury Fields in London.

Clout Shooting is another form of archery with ancient traditions, where the target is marked out on the ground and is shot at from much greater distances than in Target Archery. The distances are measured by the 'score' of yards, and today they are nine score – 180 yards – for gentlemen, and seven score – 140 yards – for ladies. The centre of the target is marked by a brightly coloured flag twelve inches square and from this point five scoring rings are measured at radii of eighteen inches, three feet, six feet, nine feet and twelve feet. Arrows falling within these rings count 5, 4, 3, 2 and 1 respectively. The rings can either be marked on the ground, or a cord or tape clearly marked with the correct distances, is looped over the central flag stick and moved in a circle whilst scoring takes place.

Normal target equipment is used to reach these distances and arrows are aimed high into the air using their full trajectory to find the target. A mark on the lower limb of the bow is used and when a sight is taken beneath the hand, an arrow shot in this way becomes known as an underhand shaft. When the sight is taken above the hand the arrow becomes a forehand shaft. In its traditional form Clout Shooting is still practised by the Woodmen of Arden and the Royal Company of Archers who use English longbows and specially shaped wooden clout arrows. The rules for Clout Shooting are contained in Part XIV of G.N.A.S. *Rules of Shooting*. (See photos 103, 104).

Flight Shooting is a highly specialized pursuit with the sole object of reaching great distances. It has relatively few adherants, but every archer is well versed in the highlights of the history of this interesting form of archery, limited to the Near East, where Turkish archers in particular reached truly remarkable distances with their powerful composite bows. Modern flight equipment is the result of careful study of ancient composite bow construction and the application of modern materials. It is an exacting form of archery, but extremely satisfying for those who indulge.

The rules are contained in Part XIII of G.N.A.S. *Rules of Shooting*, and there are three classes of competition, the Target Bow Class, the Flight Bow Class and the Free-style Class, and

107. Special release devices are used to obtain a clean and sharp loose in Flight Shooting. Note the miniature fletching to minimize air resistance.

108.   Shooting at the popinjay with blunt headed arrows.

these classes may be sub-divided according to bow weights. A classification system can be operated, in which the titles of Grand Master Flight Shot, Master Flight Shot and 1st Class Flight Shot are awarded according to qualification by shooting beyond

188

Variety in Archery

certain distances set out in a table in Rule 407 (a).

The techniques employed for Flight Shooting are specialized and are directed towards obtaining the maximum amount of cast from the bow. This is materially assisted by specially designed devices which enable the last ounce of power to be coaxed from the bow, by a system of overdrawing the arrow into a grooved shelf, by the use of a flight hook to produce a frictionless and sharp loose, and by the shooting technique itself.

British Flight shot records date from 1905 when a distance of 367 yards was achieved, and the latest record of 695 yards was set up in 1974. In America in a free-style class by the use of a foot-bow, the incredible distance of one mile, 101 yards, 1 foot and 9 inches was reached in 1970.

The forms of archery that we have discussed involve shooting at targets placed horizontally in front of the archer; as a complete departure from this, Popinjay Shooting involves shooting at a target vertically above the archer high above the ground. This particular archery diversion has its origins in Scotland where the Popinjay, or stuffed parrot, was placed on top of a church tower to be aimed at by archers standing beneath. Today blunt headed arrows are used to dislodge 'birds' from a 'roost' on a mast ninety feet high. The roost is a frame, and the birds, known as 'cocks', 'hens', and 'chicks', according to their size, score 5, 3 or 1 point when knocked off their perch. The details of competition for Popinjay Shooting are laid down in G.N.A.S. *Rules of Shooting* Part XVI. Regrettably this form of shooting is somewhat restricted in the United Kingdom due to the very few masts available, unlike the continent where numerous clubs exist solely for this type of archery. Restrictions of a different sort apply to Flight Archery which requires a considerable expanse of flat uninterrupted grassland with adequate safety provisions.

There is another alternative to Target Archery which requires only club facilities and which is excellent practice for accuracy, this is Archery Darts. It can be played indoors at a minimum distance of fifteen yards, and matches can be arranged with regular darts players. For this pastime standard archery darts faces can be obtained from archery stockists, which are merely

189

109.   The popingjay mast ninety feet high topped off by the 'roost'.

enlargements of the pattern found on ordinary darts boards, and the shooting procedures (Appendix I, G.N.A.S. *Rules of Shooting*), follow those of Target Archery with minor alterations. Indoor Target Archery is a popular winter activity, and for this there are special rounds (see page 101), and special Rules (Part XI, G.N.A.S. *Rules of Shooting*).

110.   Indoor Target Archery is a popular out of season pursuit for which special rounds at shorter distances have been designed.

Finally, a novel form of archery, Archery Golf, in which the bow and arrows are substituted for a golf club and balls. It can only be played on a regular golf course, and the idea is to duplicate each of the golfer's shots by comparable archery shots. A flight shot replaces the tee shot of the golfer, the golfer's approach shot is matched by a regular target shot from a bow, and lastly the putt is duplicated when the archer holes out by shooting at a four-inch white disc on the green. Brief regulations supplementing the

191

local golf club rules and course regulations, are included in Part XV of G.N.A.S. *Rules of Shooting*. This unusual archery activity is in fact a harmonization of many different forms of archery, it embodies the principles of Roving, the shooting techniques of Target, Flight and Clout Shooting, and the improvisation of Field Shooting. When the opportunity arises it can provide novel variety in the club programme, it is a pleasant way of encouraging extra publicity and it invariably results in furthering good relationships and social activities locally.

We have described the whole range of archery activities which are pursued today – with the exception of hunting. This particular use of the bow transforms it from a sporting implement into a lethal weapon, and as such it is outside the scope of this book for reasons that it has an appeal to a part of society who would not necessarily be attracted to the happier and more peaceful uses to which the bow can be put. The use of the bow as a hunting weapon is a subject apart, and as part of the cultural history of man it has featured as a tool for survival for many thousands of years. Opinions are polarized as to the necessity of its continuity in this role amongst the civilized nations of the world, but it is our experience that those who choose to use the bow as a means for competition by shooting at passive targets eschew its use as a means for killing.

14

PROGRESSIVE ARCHERY

By now it will have become obvious that the application of archery is diverse enough to allow for any amount of flexibility according to the particular approach chosen by the individual. It has a strong appeal to those who wish to take up not too energetic a pursuit, yet requiring a certain discipline of body and mind, but in particular providing a relaxation on warm summer afternoons in the company of like-minded friends. In many instances this is the approach which is followed by family groups, where parents and children share the pastime together. At the other extremity of participation there are those who find special thrills in competitive shooting, who are devoted to the intricacies of changing techniques, and who strive for, and frequently reach, very high standards of performance. Everyone who has taken the time and trouble to learn how to shoot enjoys a common experience, and few are not able to recall that particular moment when, with minimum of effort, when everything is just right, an arrow goes exactly where you want it to. Having once shot an arrow in this way, as near perfect as can be, and it may take a little time to find the right blend of physical effort, concentration and timing, the experience acts as a catalyst, which awakens a desire to repeat the performance. This is something of what is so special about archery – its magic if you like – difficult to explain in words, but easy to understand as a matter of human experience.

If we follow this pattern of reaction a little further we can recognize the fact that the motivation to do better is already well established. This invariably involves the human necessity of making comparisons between one's own performance and that of another. It is now not difficult to recognize the logical progression to involvement in what is described as competitive shooting. Once you have a private bet with a target companion to see who gets the better score, you have indulged in competition in its basic form. Once this need for competition is organized the wager is replaced by the prize list, and the better performance is substituted by a series of results based on highest scores computed according to handicap allowances, different classes of competition, choice of round and various distances, in fact in every permutation that can be devised. The formula is simple enough in a club championship shoot, where the highest score usually earns a medal and a round of applause, and more complex in a two to four days' national or international event where the scoring requires a team of helpers to produce an extensive list of prizewinners who can earn coveted awards such as national, world or Olympic titles, together with well-earned adulation. This is one aspect of archery that has changed, in that

111.   The Club secretary allocates targets before a shoot in the relaxed atmosphere of a local club.

whereas in the past considerable sums of money could be earned by skill with a bow and arrow, today the reward for being best is the honour of winning. However we are speaking only of amateur participation in the sport, as there are, in addition, a considerable number of professional archers who compete in their own tournaments at which substantial cash prizes are awarded.

Although professional archery is somewhat outside the scope of this book, the Professional Archers Association of America deserves a brief mention for the important part it plays in publicizing the sport through commercial promotion and widely advertised competition. Many members of this association run their own businesses, which are directly connected with archery, and others are managers of pro-shops in indoor archery lanes. A few are referees at the large indoor tournaments, and about half act as instructors at archery lanes in their own establishments and in clubs and camps. Therefore they provide an extremely valuable service to archery by their promotional and training

112.   The concentration and calm determination of competitive archery.

195

activities. There are professional archers in other countries who largely perform the same functions. In accordance with the ruling embodied in the eligibility code of the Olympic Committee, professional archers are excluded from competing at the Games.

How can a novice find out for himself whether or not he is championship material? This is a very individual matter, but sound advice would begin by a warning – do not be over-anxious to reach the top too quickly. It is a climb which becomes progressively steeper, and a slippery slope which requires a very firm footing. So many times, novices, finding that they are progressing rapidly in the familiar surroundings of their own clubs, aim too high and experience disappointment when they fail to produce the results they expected in unfamiliar surroundings at top level tournaments.

Most large meetings are open to newcomers, provided of course that competitors are affiliated to the proper authority, and entrants frequently find themselves competing with archers above their class. This is not a bad thing if you are prepared for such competition. On the other hand it is somewhat discouraging to find that you are completely outclassed without some form of prior warning. To be effective for the individual the system has to be used rationally. It is a good principle to ensure that you have reached a reasonably satisfactory standard of shooting and possibly secured your first classification or club award before entering a tournament. In other words choose your first tournament very carefully and enter the class of competition in which you know that you are competent.

To some people the first archery meeting can be a worry. For a beginner it is somewhat distracting to find yourself at a strange shooting field, having to contend with unfamiliar routines, and what can be even more unsettling, target companions who are strangers – to begin with at any rate. Add to this a preoccupation with your own carefully practised shooting techniques which have to be brought into play, and the combined effect can produce a depressing dozen or so arrows at the start of the round. However, once the nervous apprehension has been mastered, your target companions are no longer strangers and you

113.   The annual schools inter-team championship organized by the Association
        for Archery in Schools.

suddenly discover that everything begins to work in your favour.
This settling down period at the beginning of a tournament is a

problem which all archers have had to face at one time or another and many still have to overcome even after years of shooting experience. Once you have passed beyond this point it is then that you will really begin to enjoy your shooting. What is important for the newcomer is to get the experience of tournaments without worrying about scores, initially at any rate. Look upon your first two or three meetings as part of your training as a competitive archer.

There is ample scope for attending an organized competition either at club, county, regional or national level. For example, in the United Kingdom between April and October no less than 170 open tournaments were advertised for 1977. In addition there are special club meetings and a few meetings which have some restrictions as to entry, such as by the process of selection, where certain archers are chosen to represent their club, county or other organization, because of their consistently high scores. Although the places on the shooting line at international tournaments are relatively scarce, they do have to be filled, and new names constantly appear in the World Championship and Olympic results lists. There is no reason to doubt the possibility that someone, reading this book as his or her introduction to archery, will be a member of the next Olympic team. We mentioned in an earlier chapter the fact that the championship class includes archers much younger than before and champions in their teens have now become commonplace.

A brief analysis of the results of World Championship meetings over the past twenty years reveals an acceleration of individual prowess over this period, and at nearly every major tournament performances are improved generally. The championships are based on the scores for double FITA Rounds for which the maximum possible score is 2880, where every arrow finishes up in the inner gold. No archer has yet achieved this perfect result, although each successive year shows scores coming closer to perfection. The present record is 2548, which is 88·47% of maximum. However, this is one man's score from one event, and it cannot indicate general trends. A clearer overall picture of progressive improvement by the leading archers can be gained by examining the results produced by top ladies and gentlemen at World Championships over two decades. In 1956 the best archers were achieving approximately 74% of maximum, in 1966 this had risen to 81·5%, and in 1976 the best average was in the order of 86% of possible. Thus in twenty years an additional improvement in performance had risen by approximately 12%. In practical terms this improvement indicates that, theoretically, an equivalent of over half the arrows shot in a double FITA Round were taken out of the 9 zone and were more accurately shot into the 10 zone over a twenty year period. Various sets of figures could be prepared which would all lead to the same conclusion, the fact that the improvement in shooting has been consistent over the years and is still improving. This is due firstly to a keener interest by the archer himself to understand his equipment and to use it more effectively, secondly to the response by manufacturers to the increasing demand for better bows and arrows and the research and development which this has occasioned since World War Two, and finally it is in no small way due to the rapidly growing international popularity of archery through F.I.T.A. and its member associations.

Regrettably publicity has played a very small part in the popularisation of archery in recent years for a significant reason, the fact that archery is not a spectator sport. For the non-participant it offers little in the way of excitement to watch, and, as the media follow those activities which appeal to the greatest majority of the public, archery has had to take a very minor role in the sports pages of newspapers and on television. In recent years strenuous efforts have been made to improve the coverage given to major championship meetings, but with little success. However, the finest publicity that can be provided for archery is through local newsmedia. An account of a local club's activities encourages more response from those who decide that they would like to try their hand at archery than all the national coverage. It is, after all, very necessary to keep new recruits to the sport coming forward. Fortunately today, compared with a generation ago, a beginner has more facilities on which to draw,

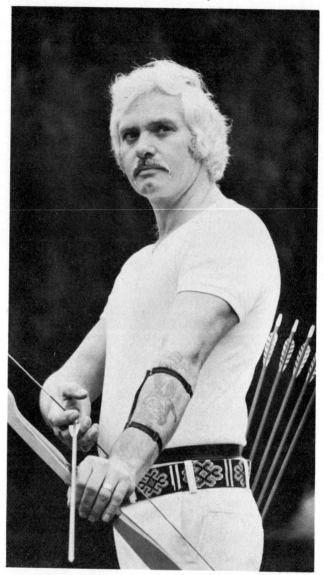

114. The competitive archer concentrates on the target with the confidence of well practised techniques behind him — momentarily isolated from outside distractions.

115. More on the spot television interviews, like this one, would help publicize the sport.

and is encouraged to develop on methodical lines rather than haphazardly going his own way – a course which more often than not leads to frustration and the pursuit of an alternative sport. Archery is complex, and unless one is specially gifted or particularly dedicated, it is not easy to master in the short term. However, with the proper guidance to overcome initial problems the whole process becomes straightforward, and the way is clear for unlimited enjoyment in the use of the bow as an ideal antidote for the hurley-burley of modern times.

In our introductory chapter we identified a number of reasons which had been given for pursuing archery in the past. Many of those reasons were based on fashion, romanticism, the need for physical fitness and half-understood concepts of psychology. In the modern world society gives in easily to artificial remedies and cure-alls for the traumatic conditions of the present day. On the other hand contemporary society is better informed than ever before, and many people are able to counterbalance the complexities of living by resorting to gentler and more practical remedies than some others which are habit forming and harmful. The

116.   Targets at 100 yards and at 80 yards at the Grand National Archery Meeting held on the same ground at Oxford for over half a century.

concept of work being a relaxant is so abstract that it is not too well understood by most people, and McKinney has described the potential benefits of archery in this context by the biophysical value of muscular activity. Emotional tension seems to be cumulative in nature and psychiatrists indicate that there is a positive value in having a socially acceptable safety valve. We all know only too well the result of psychologic tension in one day, and we have all felt tired and tense after a particularly frustrating day when everything goes wrong. Physical work of any type has the potential to relax a human being, and archery requires just the right amount of physical exertion for this purpose. There is an added psychological benefit if this exercise is performed amongst friends who are engaged in the same therapeutic ritual. Without knowing how shooting in a bow performed this magic, our ancestors organized themselves into societies and shot millions of arrows at targets for the sheer pleasure and relaxation it gave them, experiencing that feeling of well-being which today, with the help of science, we can explain more rationally. However, no matter how it is explained, or for that matter even if it is not, the pleasure of shooting can be enjoyed by anyone who cares to take the trouble to try.

Archery is a very special pastime and one which, like any other art, is specially rewarding to the individual who becomes involved. Therefore, our final advice is, take up the bow, no matter how strange it may seem to begin with, disregard age, handicap and other seemingly difficult barriers, and you will be assured of a long and very happy association with a unique leisure pastime.

GLOSSARY

ALLOW: To aim an arrow somewhat to windward to compensate for drift.

ALLOWANCE: (1) The degree or amount of divergence of aim to windward, (2) A scoring value given to provide equality of opportunity against a better archer.

ANCHOR-POINT: A fixed point to which the archer brings his shaft-hand at full draw, usually the jaw.

ARCHER'S PARADOX: The fact that an arrow which is properly shot will fly in the line of aim although the string propelling it does not quite follow that line. The point of the arrow appears to be forced away from the side of the bow; the arrow bends on release and as it passes the bow it returns to its proper line of flight.

ARCHERY DARTS: In which a special target face is used, the rules are the same as regular darts.

ARCHERY GOLF: Played on a regular golf course where the bow and arrows are substituted for golfer's club and balls.

ARROW: A projectile missile shot from a bow.

ARROW-HEAD: The striking end of an arrow usually a separate part made of steel applicable to hunting or war arrows.

ARROW PLATE: An insertion of hard material to take the chafing of a passing arrow, particularly on longbows.

ARROW REST: A projection on the side of the bow on which the arrow is laid and drawn across. (Not used on longbows).

ARROW SHELF: The lower cut-away portion of the centre section of a bow.

ARTIFICIAL POINT-OF-AIM: A mark placed on the ground at which to aim with the point of the arrow instead of using a mark on the bow or bowsight.

ASCHAM (pro. Askam): (1) A tall narrow cupboard for bows and arrows. (2) – Roger, 1515-1568, author of *Toxophilus* (1545).

BACK: (1) The side that becomes convexed when a bow is braced. (2) To attach, glued or otherwise, a strip of elastic material to the convex side of a bow as a refinement for extra strength or better performance.

BACKING: The material with which the bow is reinforced.

BELLY: The side of a bow which becomes concave when braced.

BEST GOLD: The shot nearest the exact centre of the Gold, for which a prize is often given at a tournament.

BLACK: The fourth circle of the target, coloured black, which if hit counts 3.

BLUNT: An arrow having a blunt head used for hunting small game and used in Popinjay Shooting.

BLUE: The third circle of the target, coloured blue, which if hit counts 5.

BOSS: The base on which coloured target faces are fixed. Made of a rope of straw coiled and sewn tightly.

BOUNCER: An arrow which bounces off a target.

BOW: (1) A weapon made of a supple piece of wood or other material with a cord to connect the two ends when bent, by means of which an arrow is propelled. (2) A unit of measurement of six feet used in Clout Shooting.

BOW ARM: The arm used to support the bow.

BOW CASE: A special durable covering for bows.

BOW HAND: The hand that grasps the bow handle.

BOWMAN: Applied to any person who uses archery tackle.

BOW SIGHT: Any device placed on the bow by which an archer can aim directly at the mark.

BOW STAVE: A roughly trimmed length of wood from which a complete bow is fashioned. Not joined in the centre like a pair of billets.

BOW WEIGHT: The poundage required to draw the string back the full length of the arrow.

BOW WINDOW: The space, if any, seen between the string and the side of the bow at full draw.

BOWYER: One who makes bows.

BRACE: To string the bow; to bend the bow in order to put the string in place for shooting.

BRACER: A stiff shield of leather or other smooth hard material worn on the inside of the wrist of the bow arm to protect it from blows by the string and to act as a retainer for loose clothing.

BRACING HEIGHT: The distance between bow and string at the nocking point when braced ready for use.

BUTT: A mound of turf upon which a mark to shoot at is placed, also used to describe a similar structure of bales of straw.

BUTTS: A range for target shooting.

CAST: The velocity which a bow can impart to an arrow.

CLICKER: A device fixed to the bow to give warning of overdrawing.

CLOUT: The early use of the term was applied to a white cloth placed on the ground as a marker in long distance shooting, now a form of shooting at a target on the ground at 140-180 yards.

COCK FEATHER: A feather placed at right angles to the arrow nock, usually of a different colour to ensure proper placement of the arrow on the string. (N.B. other feathers are not called hen feathers, but shaft feathers.)

COMPOSITE BOW: A bow composed of more than one material, ancient composite bows were made of wood, horn, sinews and glue, modern composite bows comprise layers of fibre-glass on a wooden core.

COMPOUND BOW: Non-conventional bow which employs a system of pulleys over which runs an extra long string to assist energy storing.

CREEPING: A slight edging forward of the fully drawn arrow immediately before the loose.

CRESTING: The colour scheme applied to the shaft forward of the fletching to identify its owner.

DOZEN: Two ends of 6 arrows. Each dozen is totalled separately.

DRAW: (1) To pull out of a given position. (2) The distance between back of bow and string in the act of shooting.

DRAWING ARM: The arm that draws the string back.

DRAWING HAND: The hand of the drawing arm, also called shaft hand.

DRIFT: Deviation in an arrow's flight caused by wind.

DRY RELEASE: To release a string without an arrow having been first placed in position, often injurious to the bow.

END: In target shooting six arrows are shot in groups of three, this is known as an end. There are slight variations in this arrangement according to the type of round shot.

FACE: Short for target face.

FAST: (1) Warning cry to any person approaching danger area. (2) A command to archers to stop shooting.

FEATHERING: The vanes of an arrow, can be feathers or made of other materials such as plastic.

FIBRE-GLASS BOW: Made entirely from fibre-glass.

FIELD CAPTAIN: In charge of shooting, responsible to the Judge.

FIELD SHOOTING: Targets with animal figures or black and white circles at marked or unmarked distances.

F.I.T.A.: Fédération Internationale Tir à l'Arc, the world governing body for archery.

FLEMISH LOOSE: A loose employing two fingers.

FLETCH: To fit an arrow with vanes.

FLETCHER: (1) An arrow maker. (2) One who fits an arrow with vanes.

FLETCHING: See Feathering.

FLIGHT SHOOTING: Shooting for the greatest distance without regard to a target.

FLIRT: An arrow which jumps out of line in flight.

FOLLOW THE STRING: Of a bow which has become curved towards the belly from use.

FOLLOW THROUGH: The act of maintaining the shooting position until the arrow strikes the mark or target.

Glossary

FOREHAND SHAFT: An arrow shot with the point-of-aim above the bow hand.

G.N.A.S.: Grand National Archery Society, a limited liability company incorporated in 1977, the governing body for archery in the United Kingdom.

GOLD: The central ring of the target painted yellow (formerly gilded) which if hit counts 9.

GREEN: A miss, or hit in the grass.

GROUND QUIVER: An upright receptacle on the ground or floor to hold an archer's arrows whilst shooting.

GROUP: Applied to a number of arrows placed in close proximity on the target.

HANDICAP: A term applied to competitive archery in which a disadvantage is imposed upon superior archers by a score allowance given to inferior archers.

HANGER: An arrow making such a shallow penetration of the target that it hangs down by its own weight.

HIT: To strike the scoring area of the target.

HOLD: A pause at full draw before loosing.

INDIRECT AIM: Aim taken by disregarding the target and using a point-of-aim.

INSTINCTIVE SHOOTING: Shooting without the aid of a sighting device, used to a large extent in Field Shooting and hunting.

JUDGE: Has overall command of shooting at an archery meeting.

KICK: A jar to the bow hand by a loosed bow, usually denotes faulty construction.

KISSER: A button on the bowstring touched by the lips at full draw to fix the elevation of the arrow.

LADY PARAMOUNT: The patroness of an archery tournament. She is the final arbiter in case of dispute and presents the prizes.

LAMINATED: Describing a bow which is made up of several layers of wood, or wood and plastics.

LET DOWN: To stop at full draw without loosing and then slowly releasing the tension.

LIMB: Two parts of a bow from the handle to the tip, known as 'upper limb' and 'lower limb'.

LINE OF FLIGHT: Path of an arrow viewed from above.

LINE OF SIGHT: Straight line between eye, sighting device and aiming mark.

LONGBOW: Traditional type of English bow usually made from a single stave of wood which as a target bow went out of general use from about 1936.

LOOSE: The act of releasing the drawn bowstring.

MARK: The object at which an arrow is shot.

MEDITERRANEAN: The three-fingered loose.

NOCK: (1) Notches in the bow tips to accommodate the string. (2) A slot in the end of the arrow in which the string fits. (3) The act of fitting an arrow to the string.

NOCKING POINT: The place on the string where an arrow should be nocked, usually marked with a raised wrapping.

OVERBOWED: Shooting with a bow that is too strong.

PERFECT END: Six consecutive arrows in the gold, also known as a Six Gold End.

PETTICOAT: The edge of the target face outside the scoring areas.

PILE: A socketed arrow-head without cutting edges used for target shooting.

PINHOLE: The exact centre of the target.

POINT-OF-AIM: An object other than the target at which the arrow is pointed in order to achieve correct elevation.

POPINJAY SHOOTING: Shooting at stuffed or dummy birds set high on a pole.

PRINCE'S RECKONING: The evaluation of hits on a standard target as: gold-9, red-7, blue-5, black-3, white-1; prescribed in 1792 by the Prince of Wales and adopted as standard in 1844 at the Grand National Meeting at York.

QUIVER: A device for holding arrows, slung at the archer's side or carried across the back for hunting and Field Shooting.

RECURVE: A curve in the limbs of a bow away from the string when unbraced, which is carefully planned to provide maximum efficiency in modern bows.

RELEASE: Same as Loose.

ROUND: A specified number of arrows shot at prescribed distances.

SELF BOW: Made of one piece of wood.

SERVING: A wrapping of thread, usually silk or linen, for about six inches at the centre of the bowstring providing a smooth surface for the fingers at the same time protecting the string from chafing.

SHAFT: The main portion of the arrow; an arrow.

SHAFT ARM, SHAFT HAND: Drawing arm, drawing hand.

SHOOT IN A BOW: The correct expression for the practice of archery, Old English suggesting that the body is framed in the bow and string at full draw.

SHOOTING GLOVE: A glove worn on the shaft hand having reinforced finger-tips.

SHOOTING LINE: The line from which the archers shoot which is straddled, parallel to the target line.

SIGHT: An adjustable device placed on the bow which enables the archer to sight at the gold at all distances.

SIX GOLD BADGE: Awarded for a perfect end.

SCATTER: An end of arrows unevenly distributed over the target and/or the ground.

SNAKE: Applied to an arrow which has worked under the grass or leaves.

SPINE: A measurement of the degree of springiness of an arrow.

STABILIZERS: A system of weights added to the bow to increase stability and to prevent the bow twisting when shot.

STRING: (1) A bowstring. (2) To fit a bow with a string.

STRINGER: A maker or seller of bowstrings.

SWEET: Said of a bow which is easy in the hand and does not kick.

TAB: A flat piece of leather to protect the drawing fingers which is slotted for the arrow nock.

TACKLE: The complete equipment of an archer.

TARGET: A standard target consists of a boss and a 4 ft diameter face divided into a central gold and four concentric rings, red, blue, black and white, or divided into 10 zones where each colour is halved for international competition.

TARGET CAPTAIN: The third archer to shoot on a target, he is responsible for recording scores for all those shooting on that target.

TARGET DAY: Any day and time appointed under the rules of a club for shooting a pre-determined round for which scores are officially recorded, as opposed to casual practice.

TARGET STAND: A wooden frame, usually three-legged, on which the target is set.

TASSEL: A large tassel of coloured yarn worn on the belt and used to clean arrows, often made in club colours.

TRAJECTORY: The path of a flying arrow.

UNDERBOWED: Provided with too weak a bow for the distance shot.

UNDERHAND SHAFT: An arrow shot with the target seen under the bow hand, as in long distance shooting.

WHITE: The fifth circle of the target, coloured white, which if hit counts 1.

YEW (*Taxus baccata*). The wood prized above all others for traditionally designed longbows; a stave is cut which includes sap-wood and heart-wood which have opposing properties. The heart-wood which is used to form the belly of the bow resists and springs back from compression, but breaks if stretched; and the sap-wood being elastic becomes the back of the bow.

INDEX

Index